This book describes, in some detail, ten "overnight trips" mostly on dirt roads, into the little known back country of northwestern Nevada and eastern California.

All trips area designed to be "loops". Only minimal back tracking is required.

All trips include extensive historical data concerning the country and the locales which are traversed.

All trips provide a definitive guide with specific directions. (you can still get lost, but there is less likelihood of it)

Some can be done in a regular car; a few require four wheel drive.

All begin and end in Reno-Sparks or Carson City.

This book is dedicated to Dorothy (Hunt) Hildreth-Amos, who was born and raised in Reno and has been camping in and exploring the back country from a very early age. She is President of Trails West Inc., an organization dedicated to defining and marking the emigrant trails across Nevada, and is a long time member of the Westerners, a national historic group. She is also a member of OCTA (Oregon California Trails Association).

Shiela Gaworski was instrumental in the preparation of the script and the maps; Elinor Chalfant provided detailed proofreading.

Composed and printed in the United States of America

Mr. Raymond M. Smith
P. O. Box 1195
Minden, NV 89423

A WARNING

This can be dangerous country, especially for a rank
novice. Distances are deceptive, the intensity of the
sunlight is not always appreciated and the cold, almost in
stantaneous with the setting sun, can be overwhelming, even
during peak summer periods. It is easy to get lost (especially without a map, as many do) and breakdowns can be
serious. Playa lakes look solid, but sometimes aren't,
especially during or after a quick thundershower. Then the
entire surface becomes a slippery morass and even a four
wheel drive vehicle can become mired hub deep. Primitive
roads, winding up rocky draws, can tear the hell out of
tires, and oil pans in no time and roads with high centers
(there are a few) can cause no end of difficulties.

Never venture into the Nevada Outback without a properly
functioning vehicle. Although it is preferable to have a
four wheel drive, it is not mandatory, (in most cases) but
whatever it is, it must me in perfect condition. Extra
tires, fan belts, hoses and fuel pumps are good insurance.
Extra oil and ample water, both for drinking and use in the
radiator is essential. Heavy jacks, a "come-a-long", some
wood blocks (old belting works well), as well as a shovel
and other tools are a necessity. Don't forget a heavy coat
or some sweaters and a wide brimmed hat. And bring some
extra food (you can always bring it back if you don't need
it).

A few driving tips:

    1. Don't try to break any speed records. The country is
meant to be seen and enjoyed; drive slowly and see it. (you
may not be back).

    2. Don't go wandering off a traveled way. This can be
disastrous and you can really become "lost" in a hurry.

    3. Don't go if the weather is bad (or threatening) or
if it has recently rained (or snowed). It can be miserable
when it is muddy. And I mean really miserable!

    4. Stay with the vehicle if you develop car trouble.
The car is easier to spot (from the air) than you are.

    5. Bring maps: USGS are good ones. This is a valuable
addition and it makes all trips more enjoyable since you
know (in advance) where you are going and what you will
see. It also helps you remember what you have seen, so
that you can impress you friends. These are attainable at
the DOT offices in Carson City or Oakmans in Reno.

6. Do not bother wild animals, especially those that are rearing young. Don't chase or harass wild horses or burros. They are protected by Federal Law.

7. Always let someone know where you are going and when you expect to return.

8. Bring a flashlight (even for day trips), a camera and a fishing pole (if the destination warrants it).

9. Don't drive alone at night (if you can help it). All sorts of bad things can happen. If you do, do it in a caravan.

10. If you happen to go through a gate leave it the way you found it. Respect landowner's rights.

In general, BLM and Forest Service lands are open to back country travel. Some areas may be closed for certain periods in order to protect wildlife rearing areas, to protect wet areas from damage, or to conserve wildlife habitat.

It is believed that the information contained herein is accurate, however, things can change in this back county. Roads can be washed out, blocked by huge boulders, or perhaps even "closed" for some reason or another. Lodging places and/or restaurants get better (or worse) inexplicably. But since all of these trips were written in the "spirit of adventure" these are minor problems at best, I hope that you can cope with them.

INDEX

1. Reno/Sparks, Spanish Springs, Pyramid Lake, Sand Pass, Smoke Creek, Squaw Valley, Duck Flat, Cedarville, (overnight) Ft. Bidwell, Vya, Swingles, Gerlach, Empire, and return.   page 1

2. Reno/Sparks (or Carson City) to Lovelock, Rabbithole, Sulphur, Jungo, Winnemucca (overnight), Grass Valley, Kennedy, Seven Devils, Bolivia, Dixie Valley, Sand Mountain, Fallon and return.   page 11

3. Reno/Sparks to Spanish Springs, Nixon, Gerlach, Swingles. Stevens Camp (overnight), High Rock Canyon, Soldiers Meadows, Pahute Canyon, Varyville, Leonard Creek, Jackson Mountains (overnight), Sulphur, "the Slate", Boiling Springs, Gerlach, Winnemucca Lake, Nixon, Wadsworth and return.   page 27

4. Reno/Sparks (Or Carson City) to Silver Springs, Yerington, Hawthorne, Mina, Belleville, Marietta, Silver Peak, Goldfield, Tonopah (overnight), Belmont, Manhattan, Smokey Valley, Kingston, Ione, Gabbs, Fallon and return.   page 41

5. Reno/Sparks (or Carson City) to Minden/Gardnerville, Holbrook, Bridgeport, Bodie, Lundy Lake, Leevining (overnite),Benton, Montgomery Pass, Belleville, Luning, Hawthorne, Schurz, Yerington and return.   page 59

6. Carson City to Minden, Woodfords, Markleeville, Silver Mountain, Ebbets Pass, Lake Alpine, Bear Valley, Murphys, Sonora (overnight), Jamestown, Twain Harte, Sonora Pass, Pickle Meadows, Walker, Topaz and return.
                                                      page 69

7. Reno/Sparks (or Carson City) to Lovelock, Oreana, Rochester, Fitting, Unionville, Mill City, Coal Canyon, Forty Mile Desert, Fallon and return.   page 79

8. Reno/Sparks to Susanville, Adin, Bieber, Fall River Mills, Lassen National Volcanic Park, Chester, Lake Almanor, Quincy, Blairsden, Sierraville, Truckee and return.   page 89

9. Carson City to Minden, Carson Pass, Kirkwood, Pioneer, West Point, Mokelumne Hill, Ione, Plymouth (overnight), Shenandoah Valley, Fiddletown, Amador City, Sutter Creek, Jackson, Volcano and return.   page 99

10. Reno/Sparks to Truckee, Sierraville, Yuba Pass, Sierra City, Downieville, Camptonville, San Juan, Nevada City (overnight), Grass Valley, (Auburn), Donner Pass, and return.   page 109

1

Reno/Sparks to Spanish Springs, Pyramid Lake, Sand Pass, Smoke Creek, Squaw Valley, Duck Flat, Cedarville (overnight), Ft. Bidwell, Vya, Swingles, Gerlach, Empire and return.

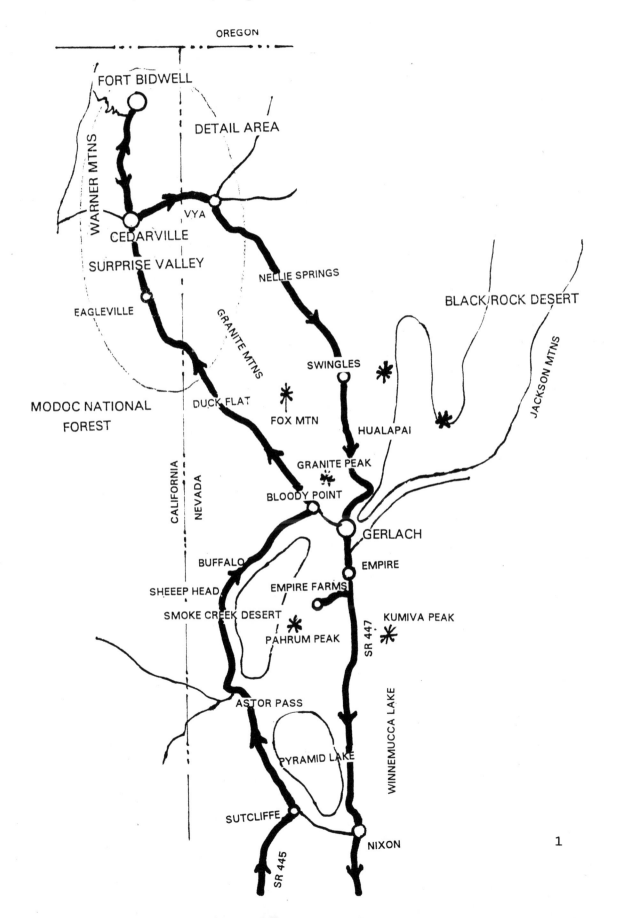

OREGON

FORT BIDWELL

DETAIL AREA

WARNER MTNS

VYA

CEDARVILLE

SURPRISE VALLEY

NELLIE SPRINGS

BLACK ROCK DESERT

EAGLEVILLE

GRANITE MTNS

JACKSON MTNS

SWINGLES

MODOC NATIONAL FOREST

DUCK FLAT

FOX MTN

HUALAPAI

CALIFORNIA

NEVADA

GRANITE PEAK

BLOODY POINT

GERLACH

BUFFALO

EMPIRE

SHEEEP HEAD

EMPIRE FARMS

SMOKE CREEK DESERT

PAHRUM PEAK

KUMIVA PEAK

SR 447

ASTOR PASS

WINNEMUCCA LAKE

PYRAMID LAKE

SUTCLIFFE

NIXON

SR 445

1

This "overnighter" takes us to Surprise Valley (California) and the little known towns of Eagleville, Cedarville and Fort Bidwell, just inside the California State Line, but only a "stones throw" from Nevada. All have a distinct Nevada feeling about them and in all reality should be part of that state.

Most of the trip is on back (dirt) roads. However, they are generally well graded and offer no difficulty, even for a regular two wheel drive. The usual precautions prevail however; carry water and provisions, extra clothing and repair equipment, including spare tire and the necessary tools. The trip out (to Cedarville) is approximately 200 miles and will require about 4-1/2 to 5 hours; the trip back totals 250 miles and takes about 5 hours.

This trip, as do most of the others, starts in Reno. Proceed northerly on the Spanish Springs Road to Pyramid Lake. Follow the road to the left (it is paved, but later turns into gravel) along the west side of the Lake, through Astor Pass, and later Sand Pass, into the southern end of the Smoke Creek Desert. Continue north through the old Bonham's Stage station (originally called Deep hole), once the site of both an airfield and a school. Proceed past Sheepshead (there is a bridge across a shallow wash with many old cottonwood trees; it is also known as Sheephead or Round Hole).

Sheephead Springs is 12 miles west. And on to Buffalo Station: Buffalo Meadows began in 1865 and was named for the buffalo grass so prevalent in the area. There never were any buffaloes however. It was the center of a large stock raising area and the site of an early day salt works and the point where Buffalo Creek enters the desert. At it's height the community had a school, two hotels, and a post office. It lasted from 1879 to 1913. Then on easterly to an intersection with SR 447 (Gerlach to Cedarville road) at "Bloody Point".

At this point turn left (north), heading up Squaw Creek Valley, past Squaw Valley Reservoir on the Fisk Ranch, and over some low mountains which leads to Duck Flat. This was an area which was heavily homesteaded in the 1920's. However, water was unreliable and most of these small farms finally went broke and are now deserted. Continue through a narrow canyon crossing the State Line into Lassen County and then into the lower end of Surprise Valley. Surprise Valley is 54 miles long and 6-10 miles wide. It is the remnant of an earlier time when a vast water body 5550 deep extended some 70 miles; even the Madeline Plains to the west were under water. The Warner Mountains border to the west; Eagle

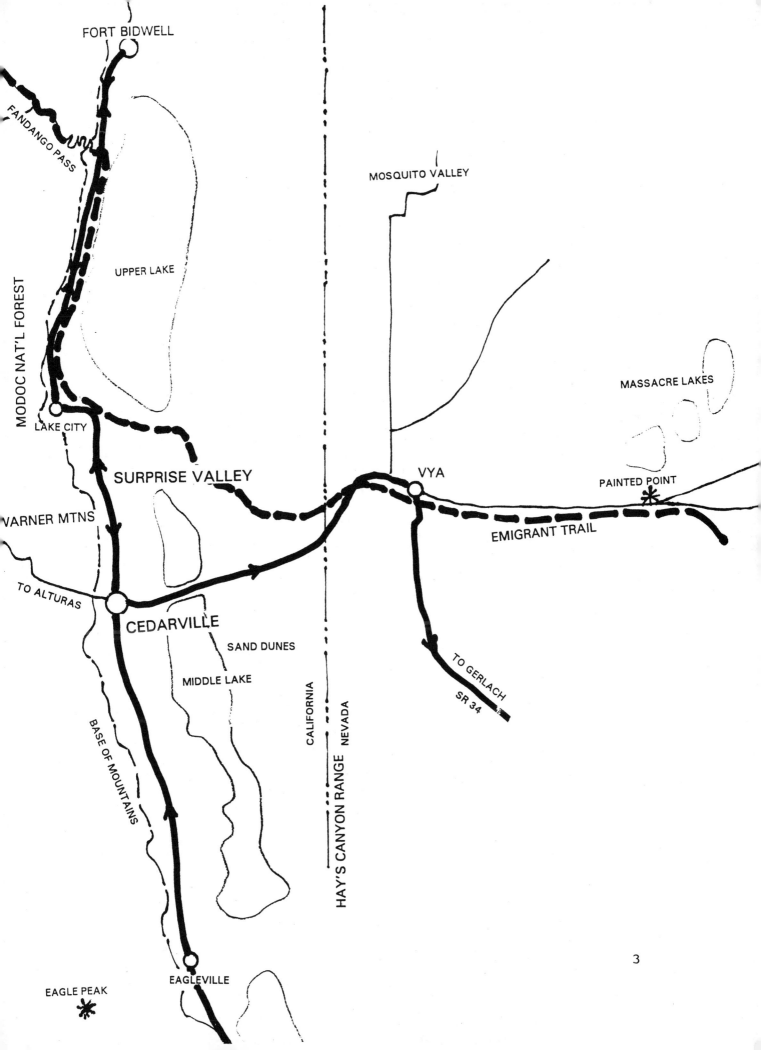

FORT BIDWELL

FANDANGO PASS

MODOC NAT'L FOREST

UPPER LAKE

MOSQUITO VALLEY

MASSACRE LAKES

LAKE CITY

SURPRISE VALLEY

VYA

PAINTED POINT

VARNER MTNS

EMIGRANT TRAIL

TO ALTURAS

CEDARVILLE

SAND DUNES

MIDDLE LAKE

CALIFORNIA

HAY'S CANYON RANGE

NEVADA

TO GERLACH

SR 34

BASE OF MOUNTAINS

EAGLE PEAK

EAGLEVILLE

3

Peak at 9,934 feet is the highest point. Basically the valley is considered to be arid and is similar in many physical characteristics to Nevada. Actually it is somewhat of an "inland island" a restricted little world of its own. Lower Alkali Lake is to the right (there is also a middle and Upper Alkali Lake- all playas) with the Hays Canyon Range behind it. Continue into Eagleville, a very small town which serves as a market place to the southern part of the valley. Continue on through green ranch meadows to Cedarville, the main town of the region.

Gas and supplies are available here, as are a motel and several restaurants. There is also the regional office of the BLM as well as a small but adequate hospital. Cedarville was begun in 1865 when the Townsend Cabin (a log house) was built. A Post Office started in 1869 and a town was platted. A general store, livery, blacksmith and hotel soon arrived, as did a minister, grist mill, sawmill, drug store, a tin shop, wagon shop and a saloon. In 1873 a Masonic lodge was organized and in 1876 an IOOF Lodge was installed. By the end of the 1870's Cedarville was the chief town in Surprise Valley, which it still is. Continue north through more well watered green meadows along the base of the Warner Mountains, past Lake City (which is no more), to Ft. Bidwell. Just before that hamlet is a well marked road to the left (west). This is the famous Fandango Pass, of the early emigrant Applegate Trail, an extremely steep (but relatively short) pull up over the Warner Mountains to a long shallow valley leading west to Goose Lake. This must have been a tough climb with exhausted cattle, discouraged people and dilapidated wagons. It is worth the extra few minutes to drive to the summit- just to savor what the pioneers went through and to enjoy the fabulous view from the top.

This town was always closely connected to the affairs of the Fort, especially when the paymaster arrived. Dances at the fort were always a major feature but the town also had a "Modoc Jockey Club" and the Bidwell Orchestra.

Not much is left of the old town, but what remains is worth wandering around for a while to see. This was to be the turn around point, utilizing the old Ft. Bidwell Bar and Restaurant located here but this is now a private boarding school and is not available for public use. Since this community is quite small and there are no other facilities, it is necessary to backtrack slightly, to Cedarville where there are now three motels: the Bonner and Cressler House, The Sunrise Motel (916-279-2161) on the road west to Alturas and the recently remodeled Drew Hotel (916-279-2423) on the main street. There are several eating establishments in town: the Golden serves a surprising "gourmet meal" and the Country Hearth Cafe has good breakfasts and lunches.

On the following morning be sure the gas tank is full and then head east on (California) SR299 to the Nevada State line where the pavement ends. There is a prominent sign which states "WINTER TRAVEL IS NOT ADVISED"; it means exactly what it says. There is another sign which announces that "There are no emergency services in northern Nevada". This too is an accurate warning. This road eventually comes to Vya which is not a community, but only a County maintenance facility, charged with keeping up the roads in this far flung area. Until the 1930's there was a general store and a gas station here, supporting about 50 people. This is all "high desert"and there are meadows and more greenery; not enough however to always "make a go of it". See the picture below.

DESERTED RANCH

A mile or so before Vya turn south (on SR34) for a long 84 mile stretch featuring high desert vistas of wide upland plateaus and narrow canyons leading to Gerlach.

Actually this is a very nice remote back country drive, which passes the Powers Ranch (Butch Powers was once Lt. Governor of California), Long Valley, Nellie Springs (a great place to hunt chukars), Hart Camp (now a somewhat dilapidated "line" shack), past Hart Mountain to the Sweetwater area where Jim and Cottonwood Creeks cross the road. There is a road here to the west, which goes down Lost Creek to the north end of Duck Flat. The road continues on to Hog Ranch Mountain, where the Western Hog Ranch Co. (Western Mining Corp.) operates an open pit leaching process, but with no milling. It produced 50,000 ounces of gold in 1986, dropping to only 18,750 ounces in 1991 but increased to 30,000 ounces in 1992. The road forks here but stay on the main route, straight ahead. In a few miles there is a fenced area containing some petrified wood which is interesting when it is realized that at one time this entire area was covered with dense forests.

Continue on to the old Swingle Ranch, where there is a now totally destroyed house and several outbuildings. Ogle Swingle was born in 1883, coming to Nevada in 1910. He established this ranch then and lived on it for the rest of his life. He helped form the Leadville Mines (nearby) and later owned them. He was a lifelong bachelor and a very independent and self-sufficient loner. During the early 20's he suffered a broken leg when a horse fell on him; he splinted the leg himself but stayed on the ranch for a week before someone came by and took him to Gerlach. He was a man of immense strength, and stories of this are still told over camp fires and in bars in Gerlach. He could lift and carry a full 55 gallon drum of gasoline (which weighs 460 pounds) without any strain, and could carry 100 pound sacks of anything under each arm all day long if necessary. Ogle died in Reno, alone in a dingy hotel room, in January 1959; 76 years old.

The road continues down Leadville Canyon past the now totally deserted hamlet of Leadville, the remains of which can be seen tucked in a fold of the mountains to the right (where there are still some trees). The road follows another Cottonwood Creek, crossing it several times on newly installed culverts (before these were very rough natural dips, which could sometimes be rather difficult), finally emerging into Hualapai Flat on the west flank of the Calico Mountains (on the left). This has become a strong agricultural area during the last 25 years and is now mostly devoted to growing feed crops, especially alfalfa. Most of the resultant 100 pound bales are compressed to small cubes and shipped to Japan. Garlic, onions, potatoes and some pinto beans are also grown, mostly as alternative crops. Continuing, pass the "Cone of Colors"- the so-called "Fly" Geyser. This is not a true geyser since it flows continually as a result of an artesian well drilled in 1916. Recent grading has disturbed this and it is no longer active. In 1963 the County was interested in developing a park and campground here but nothing came of it. Then pass the Fly Ranch area, around a loop to the east and back, along the foot of the Granite Mountains, toward Gerlach. Just a mile or so north of town, on the right, there will be a solitary street sign marked "Guru Road". This mile long dirt road is a monument to a local character (Dooby Williams) who has labored diligently to establish a "something" here. It is hard to describe, but is well worth the half hour or so that it takes to drive it and to read the many inscriptions chiseled on the imported rock slabs. There are quite a few of them ranging from just local names to rather elaborate rock edifices, many with a whimsical and philosophical nature.

MONUMENT ON GURU ROAD

Continue into Gerlach. This town officially began in 1907 when a Post Office was established although it was first settled in 1900. It was named for Louis Gerlach (of the Gerlach Land and Livestock Co) who was famous for the

7

TF brand, (mostly because he seldom used it). At one time he had 10,000 head of cattle ranging over 2,000 square miles, all totally unbranded. In 1909 the Railroad came and Gerlach began to prosper, primarily because it then had a dependable supply of water (shipped in from Granite Mountain). The town soon boasted a roundhouse, machine shop, a large two story station house, a bawdy house, general store, saloons and a scattering of houses, all built of lumber brought in by the railroad from Portola, even though the total (official) population was still less than 40. On the night of 30 October 1914, a fire burned out most of the Railroad facilities ending all dreams of Gerlach as a railroad center. Today the town totals about 350 although "Greater Gerlach," including Empire, brings it up to 750. Gerlach is, however, still a very remote community strategically located at the end of the Granite Range separating the Smoke Creek, Black Rock and Granite Creek deserts in a very remote corner of the world.

Try to plan to reach Gerlach about noon (if possible) since one of the highlights of a trip to this outpost is a meal at "Bruno's". Bruno is Bruno Selmi, the prime mover of the Gerlach scene. He owns most of the businesses in town and is the largest employer. His holdings include a small casino, a motel, the gas station and the main restaurant. He came from Tuscany in 1945 when he was 23. He still speaks with a strong Italian accent, often adding extra syllables. In 1982 a flash fire of still undetermined origin burned the original "country club" to the ground, but a new one was built in less than 3 months with everyone in the region cooperating and helping. Bruno is an institution and the area would not be the same without him. He is regionally famous for his ravioli, which he makes himself, from meat he raises himself. They are available all of the time and an order is more than enough. Many devotees have been known to drive the two hours (each way) from Reno, just to partake of them.

Depart Gerlach to the south on SR34, a paved road, about 6 miles to Empire: When the Pacific Portland Cement Co. relocated their Mound House Gypsum operations to this site near Gerlach, they named it Empire, after their former location. At first a five mile aerial tramway was necessary to convey the rock to the processing plant -this involved a 1000 foot drop with the weight of the loaded buckets going down providing the power to lift the empty buckets going up. Trucks do this now. A 6 mile railroad track was also built to haul the finished plasterboard to the Western Pacific connection in Gerlach.

For the golf nuts there is a golf course in Empire. The Burning Sands Golf Course, consisting of 9 holes, runs through town, crossing streets on several occasions. It is 20007 yards long (par 32) and play is free.

EMPIRE GOLF COURSE

Continue a mile or so to a large sign indicating a road to the right labeled "Integrated Ingredients." This is a well graded dirt road and it will take you to the Empire Farms, on the east side of the San Emidio Desert (valley), an arm of the Black Rock desert. Started 12 years ago, this original 350 acres of leased land has now expanded to over 4,000 acres, primarily used to produce garlic seed. A geothermal function was added and a new dehydration plant (using geothermal resources) is in operation. This will process some 60 million pounds of garlic and onions per year and employ a number of people, mostly from Empire. Another subsidiary is under contract with the City of Reno to import treated sludge from the Sewer Treatment Plant to be used to fertilize this desert acreage. These new operations are a model of efficiency and the owners are always pleased to show you around.

Return to the main road heading south, passing Kumiva Peak (8,226 feet), the highest in the Selenite Range on the left, past the dry remains of Winnemucca Lake (which was until the 1930's a shallow water body absolutely teeming with ducks). The Nightingale Mountains are on the far side; on into Nixon, the main settlement of the Pyramid Lake Indian Colony. There used to be a store here, selling Indian artifacts, but it is long gone. At this point, either continue south on this road to Wadsworth and west on I-80 to Reno, or continue around the south end of Pyramid Lake and then south on SR445 to Sparks and Reno.

2

Reno (Carson City) to Lovelock, Scossa, Rabbithole, Sulphur, Jungo, Winnemucca (overnight), Grass Valley, Kennedy, Seven Devils Hot Springs, Bolivia, Dixie Valley, Sand Mountain, Fallon and return.

This trip is an "overnight" (to Winnemucca), and is purposely programmed to traverse the real desert outback of Nevada as much as possible, avoiding paved highways, especially I-80, but to enable a comfortable bed and a memorable dinner at the turnaround point. On the other hand, you may wish to "dry" camp out, which is entirely feasible most anywhere. This trip does not really require a four wheel drive vehicle, most of the roads are well graded but a heavy duty car (or truck) is preferable to a regular passenger car. See the route map below.

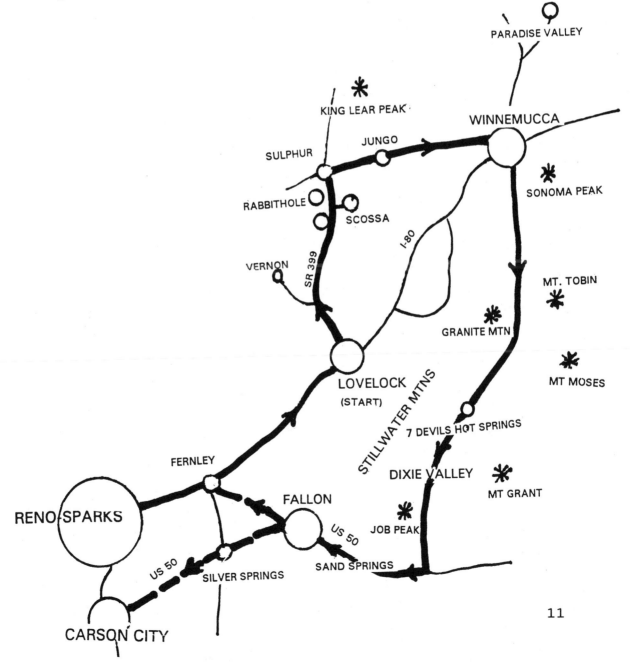

There are no services or facilities from Lovelock to Winnemucca or from Winnemucca to Fallon. Take the usual precautions, including topping the gas tank whenever you get the chance, and bring some water and provisions, (you can never tell), plus a spare tire and appropriate tools.

This trip is notable for two other elements: 1) It visits (or comes near to) about sixteen early active camps, all of which are now either totally obliterated or close to it, and 2) it traverses deserted, dry (sere would be a better term) and vacant country which at times seems interminable. This is really "desert driving" at its extreme and you won't want to return immediately.

The trip totals about 275 miles from Carson to Winnemucca and about 300 miles back to Carson City. This translates to a driving time of 4 1/2 hours to Winnemucca and about 7 to 8 hours back. Count on additional time for exploring, looking and resting.

This expedition really begins at Lovelock. Reno-Sparks adventurers can reach this point easily via I-80, some 90 miles distant. Carsonites can take several alternates; the best is US 50 east to Silver Springs, then north to Fernley where it intercepts I-80. In either case, this is the most uninteresting part of the entire trip. Lovelock; originally known as Big Meadows, was named for George Lovelock, an early Welsh pioneer. The place was important on the emigrant Trail since it offered copious meadow hay for the now exhausted teams. But the town really began in 1868 when the Central Pacific Railroad reached this point and established a station. It soon became a center for mining endeavors and an agricultural area. The town was originally part of Humboldt County , but that was split in 1918 - and the new portion named Pershing (County), after the famous General of that time. By 1920 there were 2800 people residing there, but it has been declining slightly ever since. Today it is almost entirely agriculturally oriented with 40,000 acres under irrigation, mostly producing alfalfa seed. It may also be resurrected somewhat if (and when) the newly completed state prison is ever put in use.

Seek out SR 399 (north) past the County Court House to the Lone Mountain Cemetery; continuing on this road 13 miles is Halfway House in Trinity Pass. This was a "change station"; a house, and corral serving the Lovelock-Seven Troughs Stages which began operations in 1906.

About 19 miles out, still on SR 399, there will be a fork in the road. The left branch goes across Sage Valley to Seven Troughs (site), Vernon (site), Mazuma (site) and New Tunnel, all vanished towns along the south flank of the

Seven Trough Mountains in the distance. You may elect a short detour to visit these places although except for New Tunnel, there isn't much to see. At least you can say that you have been there. It is easiest to return to the main road. Keep to the RIGHT however, across the same flat and up Rocky Canyon. The strange structure pictured below is a chukar "guzzler"- a watering station, one of many the Fish and Game Department have erected around the state.

BIRD GUZZLER

At about 41 miles you will find a dirt road to the left; this is the site of Placeritos, an early day mining camp. In the early 1870's, four prospectors, led by a "Mahogany Jack", placered about $30,000 in gold from this site on the east slope of the Kamma Mountains. This, as might be expected, caused considerable excitement. In the 1880's placer mining began using some small springs nearby. A better source was developed in 1890. The area declined thereafter, not to be resumed until 1929, when the Newmont Mining Co acquired 4,000 acres and began a sophisticated large scale operation. A camp soon took form, mainly centered around a general store and a saloon, but all work stopped in 1942 and today nothing is left. It is, in fact, hard to believe that there was ever any type of community in this forlorn spot. See the detail map on the following page.

Three miles further on this road is a trail marker indicating the crossing of the Applegate Trail. This iron rail marker set in concrete is one of many strung along this trail and the rest of the early "roads" across Nevada.

Five miles further is a road to the right; this goes to the site of Scossa, also an early and short lived camp of about the same period. The site started in 1907 with a platted town and was active for a short while, but soon faded. In December 1930 two brothers, Charles and James Scossa, two "pocket hunters" sparked a flurry of interest when they found "jewelry rock" and large scale production began in two months later with 30 residents, mostly Irishmen. For five years the area flourished and a general store, drug store, some saloons and even a lumberyard were established. Scossa, in fact, was one of the largest gold producers in the state during the depression years. By 1937 the veins played out and by 1940 it was all over. All that was left is a fairly tight house which can be a convenient refuge on stormy nights. It is still habitable due to the continuing efforts of a Boy's Club from Southern California.

SCOSSA CABIN

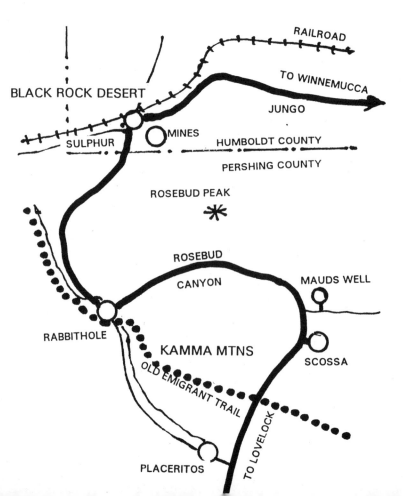

Return the three miles to the main road, turning right (north) and a few miles further is an intersection with a road from the right. This leads to Maud's Well, one of the points along the early Applegate Trail and eventually to Imlay, on the Humboldt River.

The road then veers westerly going down Rosebud Canyon to Rabbithole (site). Rosebud was an active mining area (even recently) as was Rabbithole. Rabbithole Springs was most famous as an important point on the Applegate Trail. It is doubtful that this trail would have been viable without these springs. It became an active mining area in 6 when some $3,000 was obtained from limited placer operations. In 1932, a washing plant was installed and a better road built. By 1935 there were 150 workers in the district, with activity leaching 200 yards of gravel per day. Eventually the camp boasted 28 families with over 100 men working the claims. Some limited placering also took place here as late as 1960. See the picture below.

RABBITHOLE SPRING

Rosebud began in 1906, also as a placer digging. The new community soon had graded streets, a bank, a hotel and a post office (January 1907). In nearby Rosebud Canyon, the rival town of Goldbug also was formed near some convenient springs. Soon there was a general store, and by March, 1906 there were some 800 inhabitants living there. But as usual for this period, both towns were "visionary" and were founded and promoted prior to any proof of sufficient ores to support them. By the end of 1908 both towns declined, all construction halted and the areas reverted to the ubiquitous sagebrush. There is an abandoned well and a few scraggly trees, the only shade for miles around.

Continue north to the railroad tracks and the now disappeared town of Sulphur where a new graded road extends east, more or less along the railroad, past Jungo to Winnemucca. A lone Paiute discovered native sulphur deposits on the western base of the Kamma Mountains in about 1869 and then directed prospectors to the little mounds of "yellow rocks" in exchange for a promise of a bronco, saddle and blankets which he never received. In 1874 the mine was first worked by two white partners who quarreled over the profits until one killed the other, cut him up, put him in a sack and buried him "thereabouts". It was reported that the ghost of the murdered man haunted the area until a new company came (when for some reason he was seen no more). This new operation began active production of sulfur and brimstone. They began with only one retort, but soon added others, resulting in pea-sized sulphur in 100 pound sacks for shipment. In the 1880's only six tons were produced daily (which was considerable in view of the remote location and the lack of water). The Nevada Sulphur Co. gained control of the deposits in 1899 and began even more extensive operations. The Western Pacific Railroad laid track across the desert in 1910, passing this site (and naming it Sulphur-for obvious reasons). A settlement, which included a post office, was formed and the station became the receiving point for the mined sulfur, which reached 12 tons per day in the early 1920's, despite the total destruction of the mill by fire in 1917. The automobile age eliminated the need for the local store and by 1923 the post office too, was closed). It was, and is, a truly desolate place. There were no trees, it is flat, unusually hot, dusty and without water (all drinking water was trucked from Rabbithole Springs). The town, such as it was, strangled on the edge of the Black Rock Desert; bounded by the impersonal railway tracks where trains roared through without stopping, or for that matter, without even an encouraging blast of an air horn. Today Sulfur has disappeared; there is nothing left and no services of any kind are available.

To the southeast, against the hillside, is the large (extremely large) operations of the Crofoot- Lewis Mine (Hycroft Resources and Development Co. of Winnemucca).

This major gold mine started activities in January 1988, and is now producing 110,000 ounces of gold and 151,000 ounces of silver yearly. It is an open pit mine with a cyanide heap leach process. The mine employs 100 in the mine itself, 81 at the mill and 20 in administration; most of employees live in Winnemucca and commute to work on the now newly graded road which allows moderately high speeds.

CROWFOOT-LEWIS MINE

Follow this new road east past Pulpit Rock 17 miles to Jungo. This forlorn spot lies on the westerly edge of Desert Valley, which extends east almost to Winnemucca. When the Western Pacific Railroad was completed in 1910, Jungo was established as a station, primarily as a shipping point for the ranches as far north as Denio and Quinn River. Soon there was a saloon, a post office, blacksmith, school, loading corrals, hotel and a general store.

JUNGO HOTEL (NOW GONE)

Regular auto stage service to Burns, Oregon was also established. Total permanent population, however, never reached more than about 50. In 1923, "desert lots" for "dry farms" were promoted (by a San Francisco developer) but alkali prevented their success. By 1945 only one family was left in town; they soon left. In 1952 the post office closed and today there is nothing left (absolutely nothing) to indicate that there was ever anything here.

Continue on some 40 miles across a broad, flat and empty area known as Desert Valley (most apt) and finally, into Winnemucca ("What's a Winnemucca?"- as the sign says.) There are a number of good available motels in town but I personally prefer Scott's Shady Court at Pavilion and First Streets, partly because it is on a back street, distant from the traffic noises of the main street, but also because it is "old Winnemucca" in that it resembles the old cabin courts of the early "Victory" Highway days, and it also has a swimming pool. But mostly I like it because Scotty (Felix Scott) and his wife Irene are such great people. A warning; during the summer months most (better) motels fill up early, so plan to check in no later than 4:30 or 5:00 p.m. if possible.

Winnemucca was originally known as "Frenchman's Ford" and was an important shipping point and commercial center for mines extending in all directions. In 1872 it became the County Seat of Humboldt County since it was then the largest community in the area- at 1600 people. There are a number of excellent shops, a nine hole golf course, two swimming pools and several museums, including the Buckaroo Hall (Home of the Western Heritage Museum) and the North Central Nevada Historical Society's museum (in the former Episcopal Church), on the north side, across the river. A warning: this institution has somewhat sporadic hours and is frequently not open.

Winnemucca is well known for its three Basque restaurants. The Winnemucca Hotel and the Martin Hotel are the two best known and most authentic. The third, the Ormechea is somewhat more formal. I usually prefer the Winnemucca Hotel, primarily due to its "family style" ambience, the unpretentious dining room and because they on occasion serve fresh catfish, caught from the Humboldt River, just outside the back door. I also admire the real Brunswick bar out front, a remnant from the early days when these cabinetwork masterpieces were made in England, brought around the horn in a sailing ship and then shipped to Winnemucca on the railroad. There aren't many of them left in the state since many were purchased (for very little) and transported to southern California during the 1930's for further service in private "rumpus rooms". This venerable institution was built in 1863, opening in December 1866. The present owner (and bartender), Mike Olano, has long practice in preparing excellent Picon Punches and is a true Basque character. Dinners are still comparatively cheap (now $12.00). I would suggest that you have a "Coffee Winnemucca" as a finale.

WINNEMUCCA HOTEL DINING ROOM

The Martin Hotel is on the corner of Melarky opposite the Southern Pacific Railroad tracks in the "higher" part of town. It was started as a livery stable sometime about 1880 since that area was the hub of the staging activity due to the railroad station nearby. In 1916 a new owner took over and there was a major remodeling (including Tiffany glass inserts) and a "grand opening". The operation continues today with excellent food served at individual tables.

An interesting side trip, if one has time, is to go north on US 95 and east on SR 290 to Paradise Valley. This remote green oasis was first established in 1864 by miners who had turned to farming. Indians drove out most of them in 1865, but in 1866 Camp Winfield Scott was established to "protect the area". Paradise City was established in the mid '60's as a (sort of) town. Mining along Martin Creek followed, but was never great. The town is now notable for its Fathers Day B-B-Q-, held in June.   There is also an old flour mill on Martin Creek in the extreme northeast corner of the valley, which is worth exploring. It is privately owned but the adjacent owner is most cooperative in providing access and explanations.

For the golfers Winnemucca offers a 9 hole municipal course which was created in 1954 and is open from March to October. The 3250 yard course (par 36) has somewhat small greens and no water hazards. Fees are $12 on weekdays and $14 on weekends. Carts are optional at $8.00.

Leaving Winnemucca, take the Grass Valley Road south past several large ranches. The Tobin Mountain Range is on the left. Mt. Tobin, at 9777 feet, is the highest point. Continue up the valley to the site of Goldbanks, which lies about a half mile west of the road 39 miles south of Winnemucca. You will note the scarring on the hillsides, but no evidence of any habitation remnants. Gold and Silver strikes here in 1907 started a mining rush, but limited ores produced limited success. A few miners stuck it out until 1908, but only minor amounts of quicksilver was found in scattered pockets.

Twelve and a half miles further is a turnoff to the right about 5 miles up a very rough and rocky road with numerous gullies, to the deserted site of Kennedy. Speculators believed that a gold belt connected ores at Spring Valley (Fitting) to those at Golconda. They hired an old prospector (Kennedy) and furnished him with an outfit and a year's pay to prospect the east base of the Granite Mountains between these two points. He started from Winnemucca in 1891 with 2 burros, a buckboard and supplies. Two months later he discovered gold bearing veins. In the Spring of '92 the speculator-grubstaker joined him and soon there was an influx of "jackass prospectors" swarming all over the place. By 1894 a camp of over 500 people had been founded, with a post office, newspaper (the New Era) saloons and stores. A 20 stamp mill was erected in 1895. After 1900 the district declined and today little is left of it but several ruins of miners shacks, some extensive mine dumps, a large hopper and seven rock cisterns.

KENNEDY CABIN

20

There is also a profusion of white sage growing in this canyon which is quite attractive against the darker hillside. Return to the main road.

Two and a half miles further there is an intersection (really just a fork in the road). The road to the right goes over McKinney Pass (5573') west to The Coal Canyon road just west of Lovelock. The seldom used dirt road goes south through several gates, the front yard of the Pleasant Valley Ranch, then another gate to a fork in the road. Stay left here along Spring Creek over a low pass into the head of Dixie Valley. The road to the right connects to the McKinney Pass road. At 81.5 miles (from Winnemucca) there will be another fork. Turn right, past the ranch (the left fork goes there) and then west along a boundary fence. Finally, turn right on a faint dirt track up a small hill (you will see a lone tree on top of it) to the Seven Devils Hot Springs, a very little known area at the foot of the Sou Hills. This area can be quite impressive, especially at dusk with a cold martini (assuming of course that you intend to stay there for the night).

SEVEN DEVILS HOT SPRINGS

Return to the original road, turning south along the base of the Stillwater Mountains. See the detail map on the following page. You will pass several deserted ranches which were once productive and prosperous, until the 1954 earthquake. There area several clear indications of this fault line along the road further on, which, in a single minute, changed their water sources and doomed their operations.

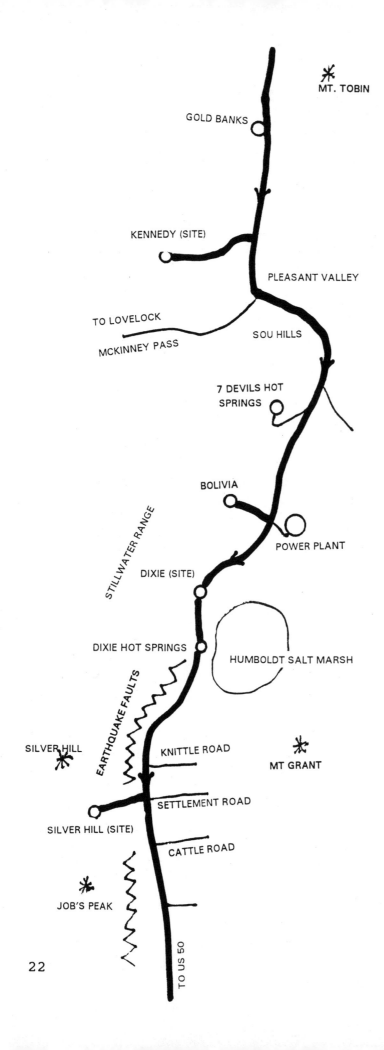

MT. TOBIN

GOLD BANKS

KENNEDY (SITE)

PLEASANT VALLEY

TO LOVELOCK

MCKINNEY PASS

SOU HILLS

7 DEVILS HOT
SPRINGS

BOLIVIA

POWER PLANT

STILLWATER RANGE

DIXIE (SITE)

DIXIE HOT SPRINGS

HUMBOLDT SALT MARSH

EARTHQUAKE FAULTS

SILVER HILL

KNITTLE ROAD

MT GRANT

SETTLEMENT ROAD

SILVER HILL (SITE)

CATTLE ROAD

JOB'S PEAK

TO US 50

22

At 94 miles there is a large new "industrial" operation. This is the Oxbow Geothermal Company's Thermal steam generating plant. Begun in 1988, they have nine deep wells (average depth is 9,500 feet) producing artesian flows of 330 degree steam and hot water. The water is pumped back into the ground; the steam motivates a huge turbine which produces 60 megawatts of power daily, all of which is transmitted 214 miles to Bishop and sold to Southern California Edison Co. Twenty-seven men live here and operate this truly impressive facility.

THERMAL POWER PLANT

At this point there is a turnoff (to the right) into a cleft in the mountains which leads 4 miles up an extremely narrow and rocky road to the site of Bolivia, later called Nickel. This mining district first produced copper ore which was hauled by wagon trains to Sacramento after its discovery in 1860. During the '70's Unionville interests began working silver veins, but remoteness to transport points hindered development. Nickel and cobalt were discovered in 1880. An English Co built a $50,000 leaching plant but it was unsuccessful due to faulty assays. Mining continued until 1890 but activity ended by 1907.

It is a pretty place with many cottonwood trees, indian paint brush and other flora, but the road into the place is for rugged travelers in rugged vehicles only. This is perhaps one of the least known sites in all of central Nevada and certainly not a place to be if there is even a

hint of an incipient thunderstorm. The surrounding steep
hillsides are devoid of any vegetation and a flash flood
down that narrow canyon would be something to avoid.

BOLIVIA

Continue south past the site of Dixie, now totally obliterated, but which was once a town of some repute. Started in
May, 1907, the area immediately "boomed" and lots were
selling for $6000 at first. Soon the place had 5 saloons, 2
restaurants, 2 general stores, a hotel, assay office and
bakery. By June of that same year there were 200 people,
but by the end of summer it was totally deserted. You will
also pass the Humboldt Salt Marsh and Dixie Hot Springs.
The road continues south for some miles into the agricultural areas where a dirt road to the right goes two miles to
the site of Silver Hills. Prospectors discovered silver
ledges on the east flank of the Stillwater Range (below the

peak known as Silver Hill) in 1860. At first, assays were as high as $1800/ton. In the spring of 1861 a townsite was laid out and within a month it had 200 inhabitants,with a daily stage line to Virginia City. The area declined but in 1878 was "rediscovered and the IXL District was organized. By 1880 there was a boarding house, 2 blacksmiths and 20 mines in development. By 1906-07 the ores gave out and the area was soon deserted.

Along here the 1954 earthquake fault line can be clearly seen in the Stillwater Mountains to the west. It appears as a line, almost a "road", where the steeper slopes meet the outfall slope. This area is exceptionally earthquake prone and many smaller shakes are reported daily.

Entering into Fairview Valley, the road extends for dreary miles, finally intersecting US 50, a paved highway (Fairview peak, at 8,243 feet, is dead ahead).

Turn to the right (west) and follow this highway to the Fairview Historic Monument (now gone), and then across Labou Flat where until several years ago, there was a locally famous "station" known as the Frenchmans. All that is left now are a few dying trees, but it was a much anticipated "beer stop" for those traveling U.S. 50, the "most lonely road in America".

FRENCHMANS STATION (1914)

Continue on over the Sand Pass Summit, then to Sand Springs A Pony Express Station in 1860 which housed a stationmaster, a spare rider and supplies. There is an emergency telephone here and an Historic Interpretive Center. The sand dunes are an interesting phenomena, especially popular with dune buggy drivers and kids of all ages.

SAND DUNES

It later became a major salt producer, mining a 4 square mile salt flat nearby. A huge processing works for this purpose was built on the edge of the flat. The Comstock in those days required vast amounts of salt and at its 1870 peak, seventy large teams transported this 80 miles for delivery, with freight bills that totaled $15,000/week. Later Borax was also mined here but that ceased in 1872. In 1906 the station revived as a staging point and watering spot (animals were 10 cents a head). The advent of the automobile age changed all of that and nothing is left today.

Continue past Salt Wells, also a Pony Express Station, (now a brothel), to Grimes Point (or Grimes Hill). This was a station on the old Central Emigrant Trail which had a post office from 1882 to 1900. It was the first water stop east of Fallon and was much used by the freighters on the run to Fairview and Wonder. It is now an archaeological area of some interest and repute. The paved highway continues on into Fallon. From there it is an easy ride either back to Reno via Hazen and Fernley, or on the Silver Springs road into Carson City.

3 Reno/Sparks to Spanish Springs, Nixon, Gerlach, Swingles, Stevens Camp,(overnight), High Rock Canyon, Soldiers Meadows, Pahute Canyon, Vary-ville, Leonard Creek, Jackson Mountains (overnight campout), Sulphur, "the Slate", Boiling Springs, Gerlach, Winnemucca Lake, Nixon, Wadsworth and return.

This is actually a "two overnighter"; the first part consists of a "luxury" campout at Stevens Camp followed by a trip down the High Rock Canyon. The second part is a tour around the perimeter of the Black Rock Desert with an overnight (campout) at Jackson Creek, on the west flank of the Jackson Mountains.

This is really "back country," with true desert camping and some rough road driving. It requires full camping equipment (both overnights are outdoors) and a sturdy vehicle (some sections require a four wheel drive) with a full tank of gas (replenished as often as possible). The total distance to the first overnight stop is about 175 miles requiring a minimum of 4 hours of driving time. The second overnight is about 100 miles further and also about 4 hours driving time, and the return trip is some 240 miles or 4-5 hours. All segments will take longer than this of course since time must be allotted for "pit stops", various explorations and some picture taking. It is an ambitious undertaking though, and not one for the faint hearted. See the route map on the following page.

Most geologists believe that Lake Lahontan began to fill with water some 70,000 years ago, during the Pleistocene period. During the following 60,000 years the last great ice sheet from the north crept down and then retreated from what is now the northern U.S. The climate changed many times during those years; then the climate was cooler and wetter; small glaciers formed in the mountains of the west. Lake Lahontan changed also. Several times it covered more than 8,000 square miles of surface area, which in combination with adjacent Lake Bonneville (in Utah) covered the intermontane plateau from the Sierra Nevada to the Wasatch Mountains. As it dried up, only modern Walker and Pyramid Lakes remained, but many playa lakes, really flat sandy oceans, also remained to indicate the original extent. The Black Rock complex, including the Black Rock Desert together with the San Emidio and Mud Lake Deserts, are prime examples of this. A current USGS survey map of this area shows an elevation of 3,848 feet above sea level, however geologic formations indicate a once level of 4,380 feet, a difference of 532 feet. Water was apparently 885 feet deep at Pyramid Lake 5,500 years ago. Lake Lahontan evaporated rapidly between 11,500 and 49,000 years ago, essentially drying up about the time humans entered the area.

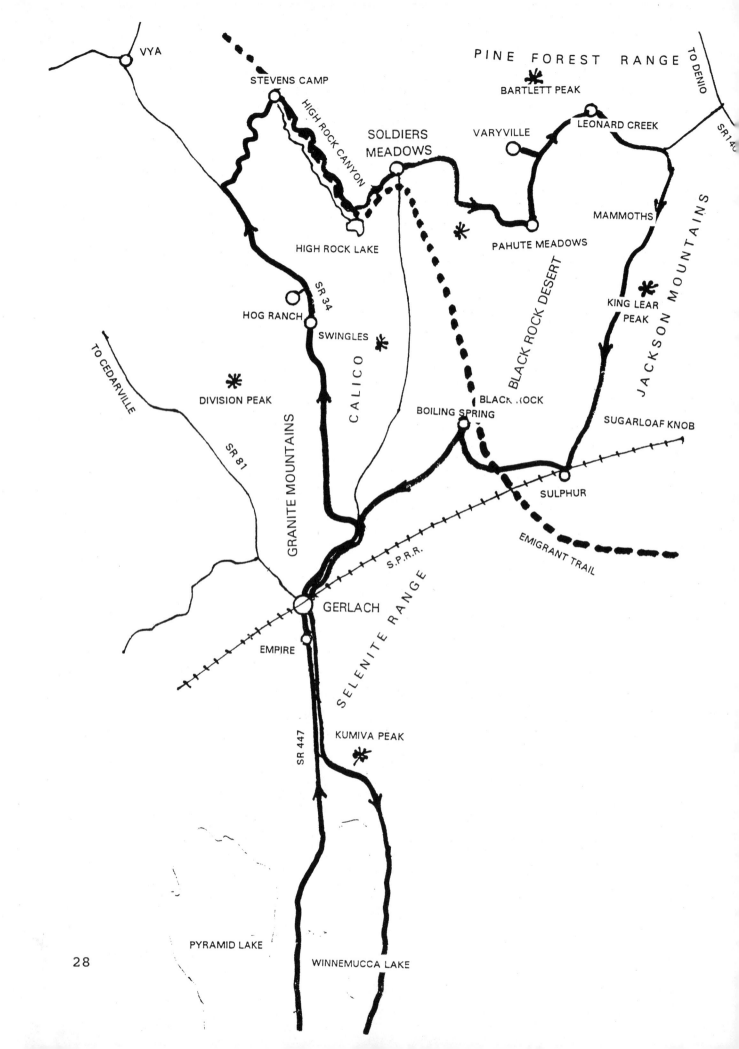

VYA

STEVENS CAMP

HIGH ROCK CANYON

SOLDIERS MEADOWS

PINE FOREST RANGE

TO DENIO

BARTLETT PEAK

VARYVILLE

LEONARD CREEK

SR 140

HIGH ROCK LAKE

PAHUTE MEADOWS

MAMMOTHS

JACKSON MOUNTAINS

BLACK ROCK DESERT

HOG RANCH

SR 34

SWINGLES

CALICO

KING LEAR PEAK

TO CEDARVILLE

SR 81

DIVISION PEAK

GRANITE MOUNTAINS

BLACK ROCK

BOILING SPRING

SUGARLOAF KNOB

SULPHUR

EMIGRANT TRAIL

S.P.R.R.

GERLACH

SELENITE RANGE

EMPIRE

SR 447

KUMIVA PEAK

PYRAMID LAKE

WINNEMUCCA LAKE

28

This trip really starts at Gerlach (get there any way you can). Gerlach is 90 miles north of Reno via SR 447. It is easiest to go east on I-80 to Wadsworth and then almost due north . This is a long, somewhat dull drive, all on pavement however. It goes past an historic marker telling of the two "battles of Pyramid Lake", through Nixon (an Indian colony), past Marble Bluff and along the west side of Winnemucca Lake, which until the 1930's was a huge shallow lake literally teaming with ducks. Kumiva Peak (8,287ft) is the prominent peak on the right at the end of the Selenite Range. You will also pass through Empire which at this point is nothing but a general store and a gas pump. The town and manufacturing plant is a mile or so to the left. Six miles further Gerlach is reached. Budget around 1-1/2 hours for this, although it probably won't take that long.

Gerlach is always a welcome stop, not only for refilling the gas tank but also a quick visit to Bruno's Country Club which is a fount of information as to the current condition of roads (especially the "Slate"- more about that later), as well as the source of undoubtedly the best homemade ravioli's ever. They are served any time, and some have been known to relish them for breakfast.

Then head north to the "Y' just outside of town. Take the right hand fork,and very shortly you will see a sign that indicates "Guru Road".

MONUMENT ON GURU ROAD

29

This mile long dirt road is a monument to a local character (Dooby Williams) who has labored diligently to establish "something" here. It is hard to describe, but is well worth the half hour or so it takes to drive it and read the many inscriptions.

Continue along the base of the Granite Mountains, past Granite Station. This is unsigned, although there is a trail marker there. This is the site of one of the first "stations" in the area; the scene of the Indian uprising of 1863 and an active place on the early stage route across the desert. All that is left are the rock foundations, but one can sense the loneliness of the place, especially as it must have been over a hundred years ago. See the picture below.

GRANITE STATION

Shortly thereafter you will see a sign, Soldiers Meadows Ranch and a dirt road to the right. Stay to the left, straight ahead, around Fly Ranch, the Cone of Colors and the Hualapai country to the mouth of Cottonwood Canyon, usually called Leadville Canyon. Continue up this recently improved road (all of the previous at-grade creek crossings have now been replaced with new culverts) past "Swingles" and the road west to the Hog Mountain Mines to a marked turnoff to Nellie Springs. On the way you will pass a fenced area which contains the remnants of a petrified stump. All of this area was once heavily forested- and this is one of the visible remains. It is a good place to stop, stretch and read the description.

At the Nellie Springs road turn right, following this dirt road over and among the hills until it finally reaches

Stevens Camp. This is a typical desert road, winding up and down shallow canyons, edged with buckbrush, sage and sometimes willows. Keep a sharp outlook as there may also be chukars; see the picture below.

BACK ROAD (WITH CHUKAR)

Stevens Camp is a relatively new cement block sidehill "cabin" erected by the BLM some years ago when the old (wooden) cabin burned. It is a luxurious accommodation (for this country) complete with running water, a number of beds, a long table and a stove. It is a popular place however, and may be occupied. It would be desirable to claim it (first come first served) not later than mid afternoon if possible. If already occupied, there is outside camping along the creek bottom in the swale below the cabin. At any rate plan to stay here for the night.

The following morning is the "high point" for this trip, a tour down the historic High Rock Canyon, the route of the original Applegate Trail, which left the Humboldt River at Rye Patch, veering northwesterly past Majuba Mountain, Rabbithole Springs, the arm of the Black Rock Desert (see later sections) to Soldiers Meadows and then on to High Rock.

High Rock Canyon has to be the "crown jewel" of the entire Black Rock country. Situated in about the geographical center it constitutes a long narrow defile stretching northwesterly connecting High Rock Lake to the Massacre Lakes area. The canyon saw its greatest use during the days of the turbulent 1850's when it was a key element in the Applegate Trail. Wagon ruts, preserved in the volcanic

rock, clearly still indicate that passage of some 150 years
ago. There are still some visible names and dates engraved
on face rock or painted with axle grease inside several
hidden caves. The canyon offers protection, shade and water
and therefore exhibits a greater variety of wildlife than
usually found in the desert. As a result of a million years
of geographic forces, the soft lava of the area has been
eroded by wind and water into fantastic formations, mainly
deep gorges cut into the more level tablelands. High Rock
Canyon is the most spectacular of these, with sheer walls
rising 800 feet from the narrow canyon floor.

In order to protect this unique complex, the BLM which
has jurisdiction over much of the state, designated it an
Area of Environmental Concern in 1984. All livestock graz-
ing has been prohibited and it is now included in portions
of three Wilderness Study areas now being evaluated for
possible inclusion into the National Wilderness Preservation
System. This designated area consists of over 630,000 acres
and over 100 miles of trails.

The canyon is also the centerpiece of a continuing effort
by various groups to close off the area entirely. A "Coali-
tion" has been formed which includes a wide variety of
preservationist, resource oriented historic societies,
museums and even some off road enthusiasts, all aimed to
this end.

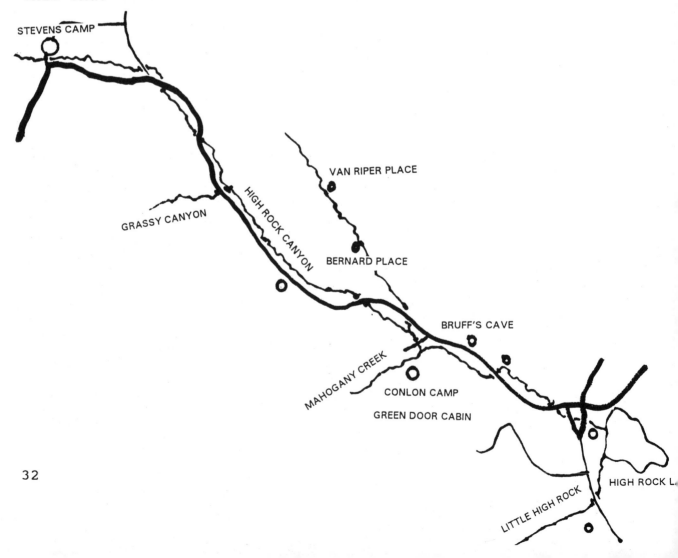

The canyon has been closed until recently due to flooding during the severe winter of 1992/93. It has been reopened (barely) by the BLM but requires a four wheel drive vehicle in several spots. It is not for the novice, but is well worth the effort. The road through is also closed to all traffic from February 15th to April 1 each year, in order to protect nesting raptors.

ENTRANCE TO HIGH ROCK

This canyon ends at High Rock Lake, a shallow depression usually filled with migrating birds. At the foot of the canyon there is a road to the left which crosses a low divide leading to Soldiers Meadows. Actually, this is Fly Canyon, the nemesis of the early pioneers. Close to the top it is still possible to see the scarring in the rocks where they had to lower their dismantled wagons over the cliffs. Once over, the road enters a broad well watered area known as Soldiers Meadows. There are many dirt roads going in all directions, but head for the ranch (where the trees are) and eventually you will blunder to it. Soldiers Meadows Ranch is now operating as the Spanish Spring Guest Ranch, catering to dudes from the Bay area and lots of other places (plus a lot of Orientals). This area, first known as Mud Meadows, is quite historic. It was a major stop for emigrants on the Applegate Trail, and later became the site of Fort McGarry and the gateway to the High Rock Canyon area, via intervening Fly Canyon. Fremont came this way in early January 1844, camping one night in the vicinity. The fort was established in November 1865 as a field camp at Summit Lake, in order to protect the mail route from Chico to Silver City (Idaho). It was designated a post in 1867 and immediately thereafter an "Indian Reservation". It had three officers' quarters, two barracks, a hospital, guard house, store house and several stables (some of which still remain). There was also a tunnel from the barracks to the stables, in case of a surprise attack. The original Spanish Springs Ranch (in California) lies on the eastern edge of the Madeline Plains, which is a headquarters ranch owned and operated by R.C. Roberts. He recently purchased this 14,000 acres and the Wheeler Ranch (old Parman ranch at Donnelly Creek), which enabled the establishment of an 85 mile cattle drive between here and the California operations. This 60 mile seven day trip costing $950 is conducted in May and in November and has proven to be most attractive to "dudes" who are usually overwhelmed by the experience of actually herding real cattle in a real saddle in a real primitive environment. There are other offerings as well, including two spring and fall horse drives (April and September) and a Ranch Buckaroo Camp (in June) consisting of five nights and six days. Phone 800-272-8282 or 800-560-1900 for more information.

SOLDIER MEADOWS BARRACKS

Depart this place on an easterly course, on a graded 18 mile road following Slumgullion Creek into the Black Rock Range. At the pass this road turns into the Pahute Canyon Road, which winds down the east side through a narrow canyon to the Pahute Meadows Ranch. This can be a difficult trip; several miles for instance is the creek bed itself. Inquire locally as to current road conditions. This is a most interesting trip into one of the least known areas of the region. There are several side roads ranging off in both directions, which offer great potential for further exploration. See the picture on the next page.

PAHUTE CANYON

This was all Indian country in the early days and several major battles were fought here in the 1860's. The road turns north, past the Battle Creek Ranch and the Monday Ranch to the intersection of the Bartlett Creek Road. Turn west (left) here, up the canyon to Josie Pearl's old place; it isn't much, see the picture below.

JOSIE'S CABIN

Josie was an early day prospector and recluse who lived alone there for many years. Her story is too long to recount here, but, is told fully in my new book (Black Rock Country of Northern Washoe, Humboldt and Pershing Counties, soon to be published).

Continue to the head of the canyon and take the right hand road, north and back around to the site of Varyville. One of the earliest prospectors in this area was Ladue Vary. He wandered the Black Rock Range for many years, eventually discovering a pay ledge in this canyon in the shadow of Bartlett Butte. He lived on the property for the remainder of his life, raised a garden and some hay. He died in Winnemucca, aged 96, in 1907. Between 1875 and 1948, the Varyville District mines produced only $108,477 in total value. The Columbia Mines Co. worked this area more recently and for a while there were a number of mobile homes tottering on stilts of rocks and cement blocks, and at least twice that many discarded vehicles as well as a proliferation of mining junk. The mobile homes are now gone, but the junk remains.

Continue down this canyon, back to he original road, which finally reaches the Leonard Creek Ranch, easily distinguishable by the many tall Lombardy poplars, tucked into the mouth of Leonard Creek Canyon, which drains a large area of the Pine Forest Range to the north. It was originally called Fish Creek (there are many of these in Nevada) but later changed to Leonard Creek, after a man who settled there; nothing is known of him. In the 1870's the ranch passed to a party named Derby who ran cattle and raised race horses. The very bad winter of 1879-1880 ruined him and many of his cattle died in the deep snow. In the mid 1880's this ranch became part of the Miller-Lux spread and in 1926, when that empire was dissolved, it was sold to Michel Bidart and Ramon Montero who ran it together for many years.

LEONARD CREEK RANCH (& SCHOOL)

Today only the Monteros operate it. This is an interesting place and the site of one of the few remaining one room schools left in the State. This is worth a picture since it probably won't last long.

The sparse winter precipitation replenishes the scattered mountain springs, which spawn small brooks flowing down the rocky canyons to the desert's edge. Fly Creek, Leonard Creek, Granite Creek, Jackson Creek, Donnelly Creek and Mud Meadows Creek are the larger of these and all resulted in ranch locations. Most are now cattle operations but at one time sheep were plentiful in the area. The first sheep operation was started by a rancher from Lovelock. Beginning in about 1883 he summered sheep in the Donnelly Mountains and Summit Lake area, wintering them in the Lovelock valley. In 1903 Carl Wheeler bought this outfit, selling it in 1907 to his younger brother. He operated it until 1922, when he died from exposure when his vehicle bogged down in deep mud while crossing the desert one wintry night. Few sheep now remain, but occasionally a band is seen. Sheep have generally been blamed for the overgrazing which plagued the Great Basin including the Black Rock area, but the real cause is more than that. Cattle, of course, contributed to the problem as did the presence of many wild horses.

THERE ARE SHEEP

Continue easterly around the point of the Pine Forest Range, and then across the valley towards the Jackson Mountains. The road veers southerly here, along the base of this range, leading to the Jackson Creek Ranch, consisting of 150,000 acres supporting 2,000 head of cattle. There is a canyon (and road) leading east at this point which, in a mile or so, provides an excellent camping spot; level, well shaded and with running water from Jackson Creek. This is the second designated "overnight campground site."

Scattered bones of prehistoric monsters have been coming to the surface in the Black Rock area for many years. The largest mammoth ever found in North America was discovered in a channel of the Quinn River near this place in 1979. Removed in 1982, this prehistoric mammal is a 50 year old Imperial Mammoth, a distant cousin of the Wooly Mammoth. The bones date back to the ice age, about 17,000 years ago. The creature measured 13 feet high at the shoulders and weighed about 13,000 pounds. Studies at this site, indicate the presence of three to five other remains, including a young calf and a large mature male with impressive tusks. The reconstructed skeleton of this monster is now on display in the State Museum in Carson City.

The following morning, after a leisurely breakfast, return to the main road and continue south. The road is good, but sometimes washboarded so do not go too fast. It is also long, with little else along the way but a sidehill cinter hot spring which offers a panoramic view of this arm of the Black Rock Desert with the darker bulk of the Black Rock Range beyond. The play of light on both results in an ever changing pattern.

Eventually the road reaches Sulphur, or at least what is now left of it. A lone Indian discovered native sulphur deposits on the eastern base of the Kamma Mountains in about 1869 and then directed prospectors to the little mounds of "yellow rocks" in exchange for a promise of a bronco, saddle and blankets, which he never received. In 1874, the mine was first worked by two white partners who quarreled over the profits until one killed the other, cut him up, put him in a sack and buried him "thereabouts". It was reported that the ghost of the murdered man haunted the area until a new company came (when for some reason he was seen no more). This new operation began active production of sulfur and brimstone. In the 1880's only six tons were produced daily. The Nevada Sulphur Co. gained control in 1899, and began more intensive operations. The Western Pacific Rail road laid track across the desert in 1910, establishing a settlement here including a post office and a station point to receive the product, which had now increased to 12 tons/day. The auto age eliminated the need for the local store and by 1923, everything was closed down.

There is an extensive mining operation on the ridge to the southeast; this is the Crofoot-Lewis Mine (Hycroft- Re sources Co. of Winnemucca) which began here in 1988. It is an open pit mine now producing about 110,000 ounces of gold and 151,000 ounces of silver per year. All 200 employees commute to this site daily from Winnemucca.

From here the route travels almost due west- out on the "Slate", the local name for the hard surfaced Black Rock Desert itself. This is a unique driving experience where there are no speed limits, no curves and no other con- straints of any kind. This huge expanse of perfectly level, white, hardpacked sand allows a driver to go in any direction at any speed. (On October 5, 1983, on the Black Rock Desert, Richard Noble drove a jet powered car- Thrust II- at 633.468 m.p.h. to break Craig Breedlove's previous record of 600.601 m.p.h, set on the Bonneville Salt Flats in Utah). It is undoubtedly exhilarating, however a few words of warning are necessary. Driving on the playa is quite different than on paved streets. If a turn is taken too fast, one does not skid, one rolls over. The playa edge is especially dangerous; often there is a viscous mud under the dry crust and if you should bog down, you are really stuck (usually all four wheels). The current rate for a tow truck from Gerlach is $100 (cash in advance). Do not, under any circumstances, venture out onto the playa during the winter time or at any time when it has or it appears that it might be raining soon. When it is wet, it is especially treacherous.

As you head west on the slate, you will soon see tire tracks veering northerly (and perhaps back northeasterly) toward the very prominent Black Rock. Follow these leads toward this feature and eventually you will find the Double Boiling Hot Springs (Fremont camped here in 1844) and a few more miles to the south is the Great Boiling Hot Spring, at the foot of the imposing Black Rock itself, from which this whole area takes its name. These hot springs are hot, at 80-90 degrees centigrade (176-191 degrees Fahrenheit), as they bubble from the ground. They are also exceptionally clear, even brilliant. The water soon cools down as it flows towards the desert floor, creating a vast marsh surrounded by alkali and sand. In earlier days these pools were popular sites for Indian encampments and later

the sheepherders utilized them for their sparse salt grass
and warm water, both extremely scarce in this region. The
road is sandy, but passable, Both of these springs were
important stops on the early Applegate Trail. They repre-
sented the first water and grass after crossing the 21 miles
of the dreaded desert (crossing at night), after leaving
Rabbithole Springs. The Van Riper ranchhouse was here in the
1930's but it burned down and now nothing is left to show
for it. There is also the remnant of a sheepherder wagon,
which has been much photographed over the years.

SHEEPHERDER WAGON

    This is a magical place; totally serene and with a si-
lence that is frightening. If you have the time, (and the
inclination) sit and just watch for a while. Listen to the
eerie silence and project yourself back into time. It is a
humbling experience, but strangely satisfying.

    Backtrack to the main slate road, turning south to its
extension into Gerlach. You will, by now, probably crave a
cold beer (or two); try the conviviality at Bruno's Country
Club. And a ravioli dinner, for which he is famous, if that
sounds enticing.

    From Gerlach it is a dreary 100 miles back to Reno/Sparks
on a paved highway. That just can't be helped.

40

4 Carson City) to Minden/Gardnerville, Topaz, Sweetwater, Fletchers, Hawthorne, Luning, Mina, Belleville, Silver Peak, Goldfield, Tonopah (overnight), Belmont, Manhattan, Smoky Valley, Kingston, Ione, Gabbs, Luning (again), Hawthorne, Schurz, Yerington, Wabuska, Ft. Churchill, Silver Springs and return.

This "overnighter" trip is designed specifically to traverse real back country in the little known central Nevada area, and also to provide a good evening dinner and a comfortable bed at the mid point (Tonopah). This is not to say that the really rugged types may not camp out if they so choose. There is plenty of opportunity for that, just take your pick. It is all open country, but it may require a "dry camp"; for an experienced camper this should not be a big deal. See the map below.

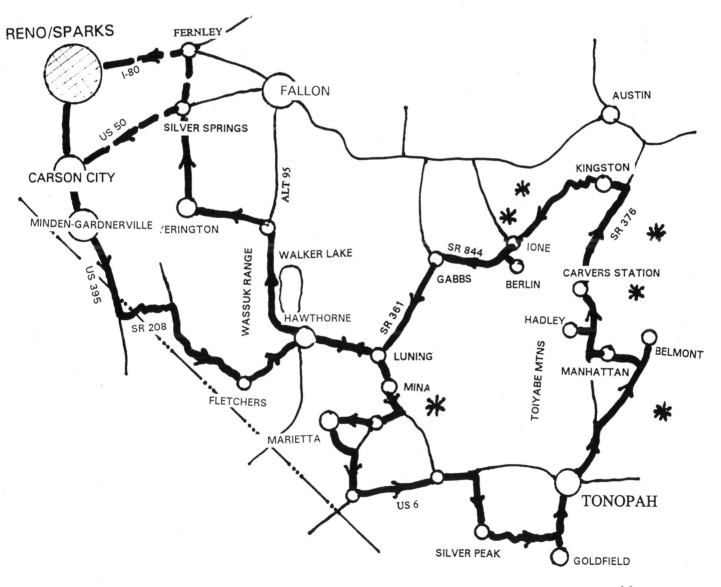

There is some paved highway involved, but most of the trip is on dirt roads, mostly well graded, but there are some spots which can be a bit difficult. A rugged vehicle, preferably a truck or something similar is advised, although four wheel capability is really not necessary. As usual, bring some provisions (just in case), as well as water and emergency equipment (including necessary tools) and extra clothing.

This trip also offers an opportunity, if you happen to be a golfer type, to play four very unique small rural courses. But be warned; these are all Nevada "outback" courses, not like the manicured greens of the urban areas.

This trip begins and ends in Carson City, which is about 30 miles south of Reno-Sparks. This will add about 40 minutes driving time each way for those coming from that area. The trip "out" to Tonopah, the turnaround point, is about 275 miles and will require a minimum of six hours driving time (plus idle time here and there). The return trip totals about 300 miles and will require about the same time.

Set your mileage indicator at 0 and head south on U.S.395 passing through the adjoining towns of Minden and Gardnerville, on to Holbrook intersection and then over a low hill to Topaz lake. Cross the State Line and continue to a turnoff to the left marked Topaz Lane (the Tule Resort is on the corner, as is a dinky post office). This point is 48 miles south of Carson City. Turn left here, through 3 1/2 miles of green wet meadows (Walker River) to the end of the pavement. Turn left on a good graded road not quite two miles to the signed intersection leading to the Risue Canyon Road. Take this road easterly, winding up a typical Nevada dry canyon then over a pass into the ravine of Desert Creek which drains the Sweetwater Mountains. The next scenic 16.8 miles wind along this creek for a while passing numerous informal camp spots (this is a popular place for people from Carson and Antelope Valleys, especially during the hot summer months), finally climbing out and proceeding to an intersection with SR 338, the road connecting Wellington to Bridgeport. Turn right here some 10 miles, crossing Sweetwater Summit (7,120 feet) to the Sweetwater Ranch on the right. The Sweetwater Ranch began in the 1860's, when it was known as Wahappa, and soon became a prominent station along the trail. A post office was reestablished in 1870 and the town consisted of a hotel, a bar, several stores and a number of houses, totaling about 50 permanent inhabitants. To the west the high range of the Sweetwater Mountains are clearly visible, dominated by four peaks: Mt. Patterson, South Sister, Middle Sister and East Sister. Continue for a mile or so to a sign indicating the road to Hawthorne. Take this road, (which is well graded now- it wasn't until recently), crossing the Walker River (on a new bridge), proceeding 6 miles to the site of "Elbow Jakes". Jake ran a station here in the early 1860's, which was only a frame house with a stable and some corrals. A post office was established in 1881. He raised cattle and ran a small dairy to supply the mining camps in and around Aurora. The East Fork of the Walker River slows down here forming deep pools in which large German Brown trout are known to lurk. The steep grade out of this oasis to the west was once known as the "Dead Ox Pitch" a most descriptive name.

ELBOW JAKES

Continue on another 8.8 miles through the Nine Mile Ranch yard, fording a small creek, to the Fletcher Cross-roads. Continue straight ahead (it is signed), and up and over Lucky Boy Pass negotiating the many switchbacks on the east side which dip down into Hawthorne. Founded in 1881 as a division point of the narrow gauge Carson and Colorado Railroad, the town site was actually determined by letting mules loose to forage for themselves during the winter. They found the most sheltered area in order to avoid the freezing winds. It became the County Seat in 1883, replacing Aurora, but growth was slow. The 1890 census reported 337 residents; ten years later it had grown by only 100. In 1915 the Southern Pacific Railroad (who had purchased the Carson and Colorado R.R.) changed to a standard gauge and rerouted the line around the east side of Walker Lake, building a new terminal at Mina. The now booming community of Goldfield got the County Seat in 1907. In 1911 Mineral County was created from the northern part of Esmeralda County, with Hawthorne named as the County Seat (again). In 1926, half of the business district was destroyed by fire. The town is (somewhat) healthy, primarily due to the presence of the Naval Ammunition Depot nearby which began in 1930, although employment there is down substantially from its previous highs. This is the site of the first rural golf course, the Walker Lake Country Club. It is a double 9 hole government owned course, built in 1952. It comprises 5514 yards (18 holes) with a par of 68. Weekly fees are $14, weekends are $16. Carts are optional at $14, club rentals are $5.00.

Continue on U.S. 95 east from Hawthorne, past extensive bunkers of the Storage Depot, some 25 miles to Luning. A stage station called Deep Wells was there before 1881 when the Carson and Colorado Railroad reached this point. From 1881 through 1882, the town enjoyed a boom with a post office, saloons etc; all thriving. Mining stopped in 1894. So did the town but the demand for copper revived the town six years later and it was again active from 1907 to 1909. It is now just a wide place in the road, but about 45 people still live there. One of the more interesting local attractions is the Long Branch Saloon, facing the main highway.

SALOON - LUNING

This is a very quaint bar, with low (and leaky) ceilings, but inside the place is full of "things", ranging from rusty mining paraphernalia to airplane models. The outside is most unpretentious and can easily be missed even in as small a place as this. This is a real rural Nevada watering spot and the owner and bartender (who is ex-navy) will talk about anything, at any time.

Continue on Alt. 95 nine more miles to Mina. In the summer of 1905 Mina was founded as a railroad division point on the Southern Pacific Railroad. It was named after Wilhelmina, a daughter of a railroad executive. Two wells

provided rather poor water. During that summer extensive
facilities were built, including a 10 stall roundhouse,
tanks, a turntable and machine shops. The town was sur-
veyed that fall, and immediately some building began to
appear. The post office came in September and by 1906 a
newspaper, stores, saloons and other activities were in
evidence, sufficient to serve several hundred people. The
town began to decline slightly in 1910, but for the next 20
years it remained "steady" at about 400 inhabitants, with
hotels, stores and service stations. The showplace was a
60 room wooden hotel, the Hotel Mina, which also had a
first class bar- "the finest watering hole between Hawthorne and Tonopah" it was said (which isn't really saying
much). After the '20's, mining declined further and the
town lost population proportionately. The newspaper quit
in 1930 and railroad traffic from the south ended in 1938.
It still functions as the southern end of the Hazen spur.

A few miles south is the deserted site of Sodaville.
Originally called Soda Springs, it was also a minor station
on the Carson and Colorado Railroad in late 1881. In the
winter of 1900-1901 it became a busy terminal and shipping
point for Tonopah, Goldfield and other related camps. For
the next three years immense 20 mule team freight wagons
hauled huge loads of supplies and machinery to and from the
town.

SODAVILLE - TODAY

Travelers to Tonopah required a dawn to midnight jaunt
across the barren flats, using 4 or sometimes 6 horse
stagecoaches. These then hauled hi-grade ore back to the
railhead. Later, in 1904, Stanley Roadsters with 32 hp
engines, capable of handling 16 passengers, replaced the

concords. The town began to die when the Tonopah Railroad
began regular service to that town in 1904 and was finished
the next year when the Carson and Colorado Railroad moved
the round house and terminal to Mina. At the time, remote
from legal supervision, the town became known as one of
Nevada's wildest and toughest, when all mining towns were
wild and tough to some degree.

SODAVILLE 1913

Eight more miles along, is the Rhodes Salt Marsh and the
now disappeared site of Rhodes. Salt was discovered here in
1862 on the Virginia Salt Marsh, now the Rhodes Salt Marsh.
Imported camels were used to haul this product to Virginia
City, which had a great need for it, until this source was
replaced by the Sand Springs operation. The production of
borax increased after 1882. A post office was in existence
from 1893 to 1911. There is a "shortcut" turnoff here (SR
360) which leads to Belleville, Marietta and eventually
Basalt. Approximately 5 miles on this road is the site of
Belleville. Begun in 1873 with the erection of a 20 stamp
mill, it supported hotels, schools, saloons, restaurants,
stables and even a newsstand. There was also a jockey club.
By 1877 it had grown to over 500 people and also boasted a
newspaper. It declined after 1882 and was totally deserted
20 years later. But while it lasted, it was a rip-roaring
hell-bent-for-leather town, with numerous gambling dives,
dance halls and boisterous bars catering to rough and rowdy
miners from nearby Candaleria and other smaller diggings and
famous for its numerous shooting forays.

Marietta, 9 miles west of the main highway was started
early in 1867 to mine salt from Teel's Salt Marsh, also
transporting it to Virginia City as well as Aurora. Some
was even hauled to Wadsworth, 5 miles to the north, for rail
shipment to out of state points. Teel's Marsh was (and is)
prone to violent wind storms which may rage for days, blow-
ing up fine dust and borax powder. Marietta became a town in

46

1877 and within a year had 150 people, a post office and several businesses. By 1880 there were 13 saloons. The 17 mile road from Marietta to Mina was a favorite arena for stage robberies, and that became almost a daily event. The stage was robbed 30 times that year, four times in one week! There are still a few old ruins and a handful of diehards continue to live there.

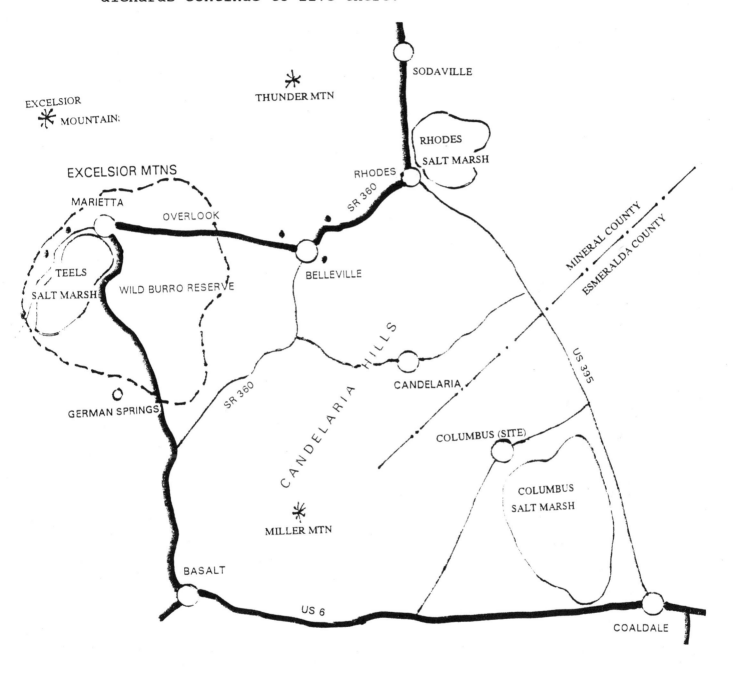

Marietta has recently been designated by the BLM as the nation's first formally recognized "Wild Burro Range". This 68,000 acre reserve supports a herd of about 85 burros who roam freely throughout the area, often congregating in the town itself, usually near (and under) the water tank. This range was formally dedicated in 1991 when Congress stated that "Wild, free roaming horses and burros are living symbols of the historic and pioneer spirit of the west. They contribute to the diversity of life forms in the Nation and enrich the lives of the American people." Actually this range is only one of the 15 areas were burros can be found in Nevada. But this area is exceptional in that they can be more easily and frequently observed, usually close enough for interesting pictures, and they are larger than those encountered further south. Burros evolved in the deserts of north Africa and parts of Asia. Over centuries, they adapted to hot dry summers, cold winters and always marginal food sources. The present population reflects Nubian and Somalian types. The Nubian is the most dominant species; it has a black stripe across the shoulders and another that extends down the middle of the back. The Somalian has stripes on both the front and back legs resembling a zebra. Hair color varies greatly from a bluish tint to shades of gray, but combinations of white, black and brown are also common.

WILD BURROS

Early explorers brought both horses and burros to America. During the late 1800's miners used them as pack animals. Some escaped (or were abandoned) into the desert forming the nucleus of today's herd.

A few miles east of the town there is a dirt road entering from the left. Return to it, turning right and circling the east side of the marsh. It is somewhat sandy at times but is easily passable. This 16.4 mile route will lead back to SR 360 (turn right there) and eventually to U.S. 6 at Basalt.

48

Basalt is only a name on a map; there is nothing there. Due south, at this point, is Boundary Peak, which at 11,145 feet is the highest point in Nevada. A hard turn left on US 6 leads 35 miles to Coaldale Junction, and 6 miles further is the intersection of SR 265, the road to Silver Peak. Twenty one miles further on this rather uninteresting, barren but paved strip leads to this place; not a tourist center by any means but interesting in a way. In the spring of 1864, prospectors discovered gold in the area and by fall additional ledges were located. A 10 stamp mill was erected and a town started. In 1866-67 "Eastern Interests" took over operations, erecting a 20 stamp mill (later doubled in capacity), but everything stopped in 1879 for no announced reason. Fire destroyed most of the buildings in 1948. The town is still viable, producing lithium and salt since The 1960's.

BRINE PONDS

Note the nice swimming pool which is the vortex of the community, at least during the hot summer months, a virtual necessity in this arid location. Speaking of "virtual", there is a trailer house on the way into town, shaded by some wispy desert trees, with a prominent sign announcing this as "A Virtual Paradise"! In the center of town, near the new post office, there is a road to the east which entails 24 miles of surprisingly good paving to an intersection with US 95, about four miles north of the famous town of Goldfield. About seven miles short of this intersection is the abandoned site of Alkali Springs. For a dozen years this spa was a center for picnics, dances and parties for the people of Goldfield. There was also swimming available in a large concrete pool. A restaurant served fine dinners. With the decline of Goldfield in 1918, the resort also declined and finally closed. Some remnants remain. This is an important focus for wild horses since it offers the only shade and water for many miles around. Usually a band of at least a dozen can be seen here.

At US 95, detour south the four miles to visit the town of Goldfield, if for no other reason than to see the Santa Fe Saloon. This old bar, originally established in 1905, claims to be the oldest "continually operating" saloon in the state, notwithstanding several disastrous fires which all but wiped out the community on several occasions. It is a classic in its way, with a low ceiling and real early day ambience. There are also usually a number of "characters" in the place. Ask locally for direction if necessary, although there are signs. There are a number of antique stores in town, which are worth browsing through.

GOLDFIELD 1906

The town also features a number of vacant stone buildings, some of which are multi-story, reflecting the earlier boom days of the community. There is a restaurant, the Mozart Club and various services, including a repair garage.

GOLDFIELD CRIBS

Goldfield, was also a "rip-roarer" in its day. The picture is of the tenderloin area on lower Main Street, with its row of cribs. In its heyday there were over 100 girls there.

Backtracking slightly, return north on US 95 to Tonopah (26 miles) for the "overnight stop". There are a number of motels in town plus the rehabilitated old Mizpah Hotel (which is interesting but tends to be somewhat noisy at night). There are a variety of restaurants as well, including a good Mexican spot (El Marques) on the north end. But I would suggest the Dempsey Room below the Mizpah. It serves excellent dinners in a surprising manner, including, if you can believe it, sorbet between courses. The bar at the Mizpah is unique as well, complete with marble columns etc., and one can usually find some interesting people and on-going conversations.

TONOPAH MAIN STREET

Leaving Tonopah the next day, take US 6 east for about four miles to its intersection with SR 376. Turn north on this road, past the Tonopah Correction Center (a prison camp) on the left to a large clump of trees on the right. This is a well field which is the source of the water supply for Tonopah. 44 miles (from Tonopah) there is a newly paved road to the right which leads approximately 27 miles to Belmont. Belmont was the first county seat of Nye County (in 1867) and a major mining center in its day. Initial discoveries were made in October 1865 resulting in a rush in 1866, drawing prospectors from Ione, Austin and many other districts. First named Silver Bend, it became an important mining, milling and trading center for everything within a radius of 100 miles. Located in a wooded canyon with ample water, the town soon had a bank, school, several newspapers, a post office, numerous stores and

shops and reached a peak population of about 2000 by early
1868. It is now a sort of retirement center and there seems
to be a number of new homes in the area although there are
now only five permanent residents. A new B&B ("The Philadel-
phia") is now being restored in an old building which, by
the summer of 1995, will have five rooms, two baths and a
steak house. A new social center ("saloon") is operating in
an old building now being enlarged into another old building
but it is only open on the weekends. On those weekends
however, business is good and as many as 80 "explorers" may
be camped in the area to take advantage of the conviviality,
music and good times here. The bar here came from the
wrecked Cosmopolitan Hotel just up the street.

BELMONT SOCIAL CLUB

    Again backtrack a few miles to a dirt road (SR 377)
which goes over a low pass to Manhattan. This is a sort of
"Ghost town," (although not totally deserted by any means)
which in its glory days was an active center. Silver ledges
were found in 1866 but were abandoned in 1869. In 1905,
rich float was found, eight town sites were staked out and
by the end of that year several hundred inhabitants were
building homes. In 1906 the "boom" really heated up and
Manhattan became a "city" of about 4,000, all within two
weeks!

    All sorts of transportation means flooded the area
roads, especially from Tonopah, and at all hours. Saloons
sold floor space for sleeping and a bath in a wooden tub
cost $3.00. By spring 3 banks, 2 newspapers, many saloons,
assay offices, schools and houses were erected and even
electric lights and water services were installed. Stage
lines ran off in all directions and the town received
national publicity.

MANHATTAN - ABOUT 1912

The San Francisco earthquake in April 1906 also jolted this town, when San Francisco investors suddenly withdrew and in less than a month, most of the mines ceased production. The population fell to only a few hundred. Rich strikes in the summer and fall of 1906 and in the spring of 1907 revived it somewhat. In 1909 the area rebounded when placer operations below town began and for many succeeding years this remained one of the most prosperous towns in Nevada. It maintained a steady 800-1000 population, a hospital was built and everything seemed secure. Operations subsided in the mid 1920's but the town survived the depression years quite successfully. Lower Manhattan featured a large gold dredge, known as the "Big Boat", which operated there from 1939 to the fall of 1947 . Manhattan has recently come back to life (somewhat) as a direct result of the mining boom now underway in Round Mountain, now a major mining center only a few miles to the north. Manhattan is also the home of the Manhattan Bar which is locally famous for a distinctive attraction called the " Chicken Shit". This consists of an 8 by 8 foot cage, the bottom of which is marked off into 100 spaces. On "notable occasions" -and in Manhattan these are frequent- these numbers are "bought" by thirsty patrons for a buck apiece, and when sold out, a live chicken is dropped therein. Whatever number the chicken "shits on", is the winner of the pot. Such is life in the Nevada outback!

This road continues on (there is no other) to an intersection with SR 376 through Big Smoky Valley. Nestled between the Toiyabe Mountains to the left and the Toquima Mountains to the east, this 140 mile long valley was long inhabited by the Shoshone and Paiute tribes. Ranches were first established in the 1860's and several stations were later created to provide for the exchange of horses on the Belmont to Austin Stage Road. Turn right (north) on this route, to the signed turnoff to Hadley. A "new town" in all it's essence, this community boasts paved streets, curbs and gutters, a new (enclosed) swimming pool, a new library, a new community Hall, a new high school and a new nine hole golf course, The Round Mountain Golf Course. This second rural course is "public" (although privately owned) and consists of 9 holes at 7138 yards with a par of 72. It is said to be a "typical English Links course", with three lakes on six holes. Green fees are $15, gas carts are $16. All of these facilities were built through the Proceeds of Mining Taxes. It is proposed to replace (eventually) the old Town of Round Mountain with this new community. Proceed past the turnoff to Round Mountain (this old town is nothing and not worth the short detour) to Carvers Station, a truck depot, restaurant and center of Smokey Valley social life for many years. It is also a mid point where gas and other services are available. Carver's Country Casino serves what has to be one of the largest and best steaks or chicken dinners in all of Nevada.

Ten miles beyond Carvers is an Historic Monument indicating the site of Ophir, in Ophir Canyon. It is worth the moment to stop and read it. The town of Ophir itself still exists as a rock remnant of the early days but the road into it is very difficult, requiring both a four wheel drive vehicle and a strong spirit. And 2.7 miles further is another Historic Monument defining Darrough's Hot Springs, the oldest stage station in Smokey Valley and the place where John C. Fremont camped in 1845. Continue north on SR 376 sixteen miles to the Kingston Canyon Road (it is signed), and turn west, up this canyon road, to the little retirement community of Kingston Village. First exploited in 1863, a stamp mill for the Victorine Mine was erected at the foot of the canyon. A recreational retirement community has developed here over the last 20 years or so and there are now about 40 permanent homes. Continue on six miles up the canyon past the Victorine Mine (remnants) to the Kingston Canyon Campground which consists of 12 campsites, toilets, drinking water and hiking trails; it is open from mid May to mid October. Continue on this road up the canyon to Groves Lake which now has water in it (for many years it leaked uncontrollably) and some fishing opportunities, and then up over the summit of the Toiyabe Range. Bunker Hill at 11,474 feet and Toiyabe Mtn. at 10,793 feet are both on the right. Coming down the other side through Big Canyon there is also a developed Forest Service campground. This is a steep and somewhat scary road and is not passable during the winter months. At the foot of the canyon, turn left (south), up the Reese River Valley past the old Visbek ranch, the Elkhorn Pass Road and the Yomba Indian Reservation to a road to the right, which goes over Ione Summit to a wide place in the road called Ione. Begun in 1863, in a pretty canyon, this community finally reached 500 people and was named County Seat of then Nye County. Mining declined by 1866 and the County seat was unceremoniously and promptly moved to Belmont -which was by then larger- and growing. The Ione mines never produced as hoped. There is, however, one great building left; a good one, the Ore House. This funky old one story stone building is the center of activity and caters to a vast (but sparse) population within at least a hundred mile radius.

IONE

This place is usually patronized by wind bitten ranchers, hard rock miners, truckers, geologists and adventurers, but only a few tourists, since it is remote and only reachable by difficult dirt roads.

From Ione, go west a few miles then veer sharply back. Follow the signs to the Berlin-Ichthyosaur State Park. Berlin was first worked for silver in 1895. Later a 30 stamp mill was erected. At its height it only had some 250 people, supported by stores, a post office, an auto shop and a stage line. The yields were never large and by 1909 everything stopped. The park is preserved in a state of "arrested decay"; several old buildings are open for inspection and a Ranger is here during the summer months. Quite nearby is the Ichthyosaur display in Union Canyon. All of this area (as was most of Nevada) was once the bed of a vast inland sea; there giant "fish lizards" were abundant. Thirty-four fossil skeletons of these have been excavated; three of which are on permanent exhibition.

Restrooms, tables, B-B-Q's and water are available at the four campsites. There is a small overnight fee. You may wish to detour another few miles to the next canyon south, this is the site of Grantsville, where silver was discovered in 1863 and a camp in the upper end of the canyon soon established. It was abandoned (more or less) for a while for the new diggings in White Pine County, but later a rebirth began and soon a 20 stamp mill was in operation and 800 people were in residence. There were daily stages to Austin (via Ione) and Eureka (via Belmont). It was all over by 1885 however.

Return seven miles or so to the pavement and then go on 13 more miles over the Paradise Range to Gabbs. This totally isolated "company" town is almost mid state and is some 32 miles east of Luning. There are still about 200 people living there, down substantially from the 800 of only a few years ago. The town appears to be heading for an eventual "ghost town" status since all of the mining has now shut down. It was originally begun as a magnesium operation, but later turned to gold extraction. Gas and supplies are available here. There is also an interesting local bar, the R & D where cold beers seem to be the favored drink and there is always a local character or two. This is especially refreshing on a hot autumn afternoon. This is the site of the third "golf course" and in many ways it is the most unique of them all. This is the Sandy Bottom Golf Course, a public play course (the only one in Nevada) constructed in 1958 and is 3010 yards long with a par of 35. Membership is $10/year but non-members can play free at any time. There are no carts and no rentals. It is located on a dry lake bed and temperatures can be extreme, say- at noon- in August.

From Gabbs, go south on a good paved road to U.S. 95 at Luning. Here the route is retraced (slightly) back to Hawthorne. Continue through this town, and then along the shore of Walker Lake. This last remnant of ancient Lake Lahontan, which once covered almost all of the state, is now only 38,000 acres (60 sq. miles) in extent and is in the final stages of evaporating due to the total diversion of the Walker River (which was its only major water source) to irrigation for upstream ranches. The mountains on the left are the Wassuk Range, with Mt. Grant at 11,245 feet, the highest point.

This route then leads to Schurz, a small Indian colony with a general store and little else. Veer to the west here for the 25 mile run through dry hills to Yerington. This is the site of the fourth golf course, The Mason Valley course (privately owned), a 6638 yard affair constructed in 1964. It is a par 72 with some water hazards. The fee is $11 weekly and $13 on weekends. Carts are optional at $12 and club rental is $5.00.

Continue north on Alt. 95 through the northern portion of the Mason Valley agricultural area. Note the Sierra Pacific Power Co, steam generating station to the right. Some years ago there was a scheme involving some University of Nevada professors who wanted to raise "giant shrimp" in the hot water (cooling ponds) here; it didn't work out though, mostly due to the birds getting there first.

A few miles further is the railroad crossing of Wabuska. This settlement began in the 1870's and in 1874 a post office was opened. The Carson and Colorado Railroad reached this point in 1881, creating a station here which also served as a dinner station; in those days trains did not carry a dining car. In 1905 the Southern Pacific Railroad replaced it with a standard gauge line. When the Nevada Copper Belt Railroad began in 1911, Wabuska became a true railroad center and a major junction point. It is interesting to note that the old Wabuska stationhouse has been moved and now is part of the Railroad Museum in Carson City. At the height of its boom during World War One, the town boasted a large railroad station, a two room school, grocery stores, seven saloons and a population of about 100. Copper mining subsided after 1919 and Wabuska shrank with it, finally offering only one grocery store and a dozen houses. The sole surviving structure - a road house naturally- is now closed and is for sale. Across from Wabuska, against the sidehill is the site of Thompsons Mill. The copper mines west of Yerington, operated by the Mason Valley Mining Co., resulted in the erection of a smelter at the north end of the valley in 1910. Actually it was two smelters of 500 ton capacity. They first began operations in 1912, treating 700-1000 tons of copper ore daily. A town soon sprung up including several blocks of residences, stores, saloons, an auto repair shop and a population of about 350. The mill closed in late 1914, resumed briefly in 1917, but stopped for good in 1919.

Then, after going over some low dry hills and crossing the Carson River, there is a green area which is the site of "Bucklands", or Buckland Station. This was a roadhouse, named for its owner, Sam Buckland. It first opened in 1859 to serve travelers on the Emigrant Trail. He built a ranch house in the spring of 1860 and then a trading post, tavern and a hotel. A blacksmith and a wagon repair facility followed as did a toll bridge. In November 1861 it became the County Seat of Churchill County. By this time corrals, a wagon yard and a farm had been added. Before 1870 Buckland also built a larger hotel with a dining room, bar and dance hall, which proved to be a most popular attraction. The large hotel still stands, the rest of the property has, off and on, been a private game farm.

A mile north of this and a short side trip of only a mile or so is Fort Churchill. This was Nevada's first, largest and most important military post. It began in 1860 with a post office and by the end of 1861 there were 600 men garrisoned there. During the remainder of the '60's it protected the developing western Nevada settlements as well as the Emigrant Road. During the Civil War, California Volunteers replaced the regular troops who were called east. From 1867 to 1869 there was only one company left in force, however by then most of the Indian troubles were over. The completion of the Central Pacific Railroad in 1868 displaced travel on the Overland Trail and by September, 1869 the fort was all but abandoned. Six months later the buildings were sold at auction- to Sam Buckland- for $750. It is now a State Park and a National Historic landmark. Some camping facilities are available.

From here it is an uninteresting trip north to Silver Springs and then back to Carson City on U.S. 50, or continue on Alt 95 to Fernley and then west on I-80 to Reno and Sparks.

Funerals were common affairs in the gold rush days. They were for the most part very solemn, the friends of the deceased being gathered around to say a last good word for the departed. One funeral was going along as planned, the thuds of the pick-axes and the shovels of the grave-diggers sounding in the background, and the minister solemnly intoning the virtues of the deceased before he was laid away. Suddenly there was a shout from the grave-diggers' contingent of "Gold!" Everybody jumped as if shot, and with the minister leading the way, made a rush for the grave. Shortly all the mourners were busy staking out claims and digging for gold, and a miniature gold rush was on. The corpse was hastily taken to other parts and buried even faster.

5

Reno/Sparks/Carson City to Minden/Gardnerville, Holbrook, Bridgeport, Bodie, Lundy Lake, Lee Vining (overnight), Benton, Montgomery Pass, Belleville, Luning, Hawthorne, Shurz, Yerington and return.

This is an overnight "getaway" trip but is one which is mostly on paved roads with only minimal dirt road driving. It is a "loop" route (with a side trip to Bodie) ending at LeeVining (the overnight stop), on the shores of Mono Lake and then back through the Mono Mills Forest and some (pretty desolate) Nevada towns strung along US 395 between Hawthorne and Coaldale. See the route map below.

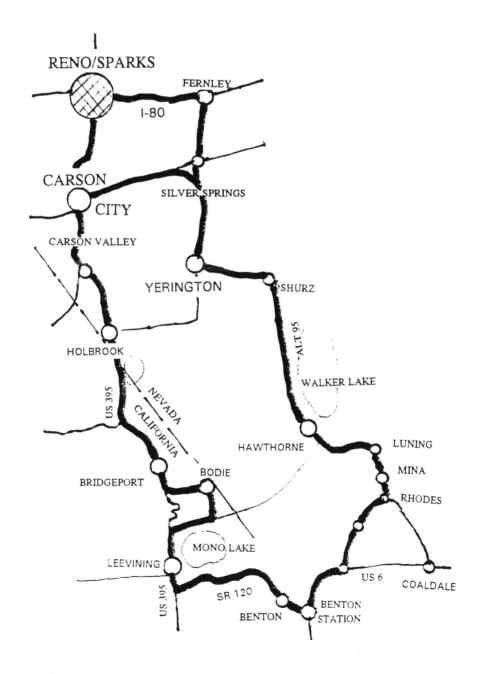

It is very suitable for a regular passenger car since almost all of it is paved. The trip out totals 175 miles-requiring about five hours driving time to the turnaround point (LeeVining) but it could be up to 8 hours if adequate time is spent looking around in Bodie and at the Interpretive Center at Mono Lake. The return trip is somewhat long-300 miles, which will require about 6 hours driving time (at an average speed of 60 mph). Gas and services are available at regular intervals, however, take the usual precautions.

The routing starts (as usual) in Reno, follows U.S. 395 south through Carson City and the Minden-Gardnerville area and on south past Topaz Lake and into California at Coleville in the Antelope Valley area. Continue through Walker and over the pass to Bridgeport, the county seat of Mono County. This is all beautiful high country with alpine meadows and some pine trees. Bridgeport is a really green oasis, being well watered by the Walker River, but has the distinction of being one of the coldest places in the west during the winter (which is about 8 months long it seems). Continue south, still on 395 to a well marked turnoff to Bodie. Turn left here following the dirt road some 15 miles to this perhaps best preserved" ghost town" in the west. See the detailed map below.

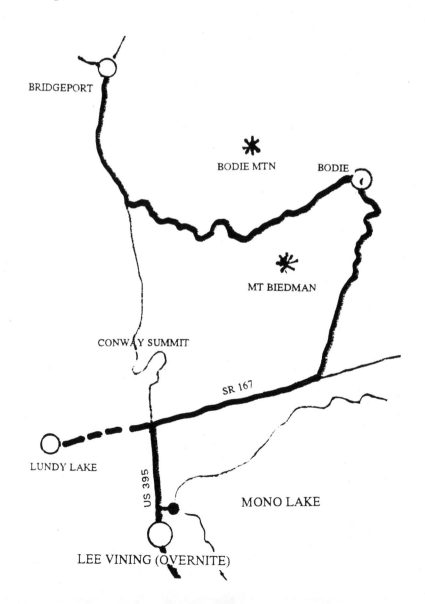

60

Bodie was a fabulous place. Located some 36 miles west of Hawthorne, over the Lucky Boy Pass, the area was first placered in late 1859, but nothing really happened until the summer of 1861 when lode gold was discovered. In the following four years the town grew respectably, but yields continued to be sporadic until 1864, when a rich vein was found in an abandoned working. There were more strikes in 1877 and 1878 and then Bodie really boomed! The severe winter of 1878-79 resulted in many deaths, mostly from exposure and disease. There was little food, little employment and very poor housing. In the spring of 1879 a major influx of new miners arrived and large volumes of freight were teamed in, relieving the scarcities of the winter. The camp was always noted for being wild and lawless, even from the start; the "Bad man from Bodie" was a well known saying throughout the west. By '75 five rival daily newspapers and three weeklys were in local circulation. There was also an active social life with theaters, organized picnics and sporting events on a regular basis. By the end of 1879 10,000 people were in residence. The town was built entirely of wood, and wood was not only scarce but extremely expensive. This instigated the construction of the Bodie and Benton Railroad, a 32 mile line from Mono Mills (at Mono Lake) where timber was cut and milled for transhipment to the mines. Ore was then hauled out on the return trip. After 1881 there was a rapid decline and by '83 only some 500 people remained in camp with only four mines still working. Fire destroyed most of the town in 1932. In 1962 the California State Park system took over the entire area and in 1964 it was named a State Historical Park. It remains today in an interesting "state of arrested decay" with many buildings intact and even the scattered debris protected against removal. There are rangers on duty all summer (one even lives there over the winter, often totally isolated by deep snows). There is a designated parking lot on the edge of town (no vehicles are allowed in the old section) and there is a $5.00/car admittance fee.

From Bodie, take the back road (not the main road to US395 on which you came), south to California Route 167. This 14 mile dirt road winds down a shallow canyon to this paved highway and although not rough will require some care--and some time. Turn right, towards the mountains to the US 395 intersection at Mono Lake.

The Mono Basin is a strange place; a place that is trapped by geography. "It is a country of wonderful contrasts; hot deserts bordered by snow laden mountains, cinders and ashes scattered on glacier polished pavements, frost and fire working in the making of beauty" said John Muir during his first summer in the Sierras. "Mono" means flies in the Yokuts language, the Indians who lived to the south of the basin; the Kuzedika (Mono Lake Pauite), who lived in the basin, collected the alkali fly pupae as a main food source. During the lake's million year history, it has never had an outlet. As a consequence, this highly alkaline lake appears prehistoric in character and appearance. There is an island (Paoha) which in earlier times figured in some (presumed) oil explorations (too long a story to be told here) and is now a rookery for seagulls and pelicans. Although fish cannot live in the saline water, brine shrimp and alkali flies have adapted and reproduce by the millions, which provides food for the birds and migratory waterfowl that visit the lake regularly. See the area map on the following page.

Then either turn south about 4 miles to the little hamlet of LeeVining. which is the overnight stop or you may wish to detour (straight ahead) to the nearby old mining town of Lundy, and Lundy Lake a few miles up Lundy Canyon. Lundy Lake is at 7,186 feet and is surrounded on three sides by towering peaks in the 11-12,000 foot range. German Brown and Rainbow trout are plentiful here while smaller Eastern Brook trout area abundant in the beaver ponds and the creek at the head of the canyon. The Lundy Lake Resort offers fishing licenses, boat rentals, information on hiking and mountain biking and also provides a general store. There are also housekeeping cabins, mobile homes, rustic housekeeping cabins and trailer parking, camp huts and camper and tent sites available. (write P.O.Box 550, Lee Vining Calif. 93541, there is no telephone). The May Lundy Mine, high on a mountainside was its reason for being. Never a large town, its greatest disadvantage was the occasional avalanche which roared down Mt. Scowden, destroying much of the community more than once. Still, it is a pretty place, and quite dramatic.

LUNDY CANYON

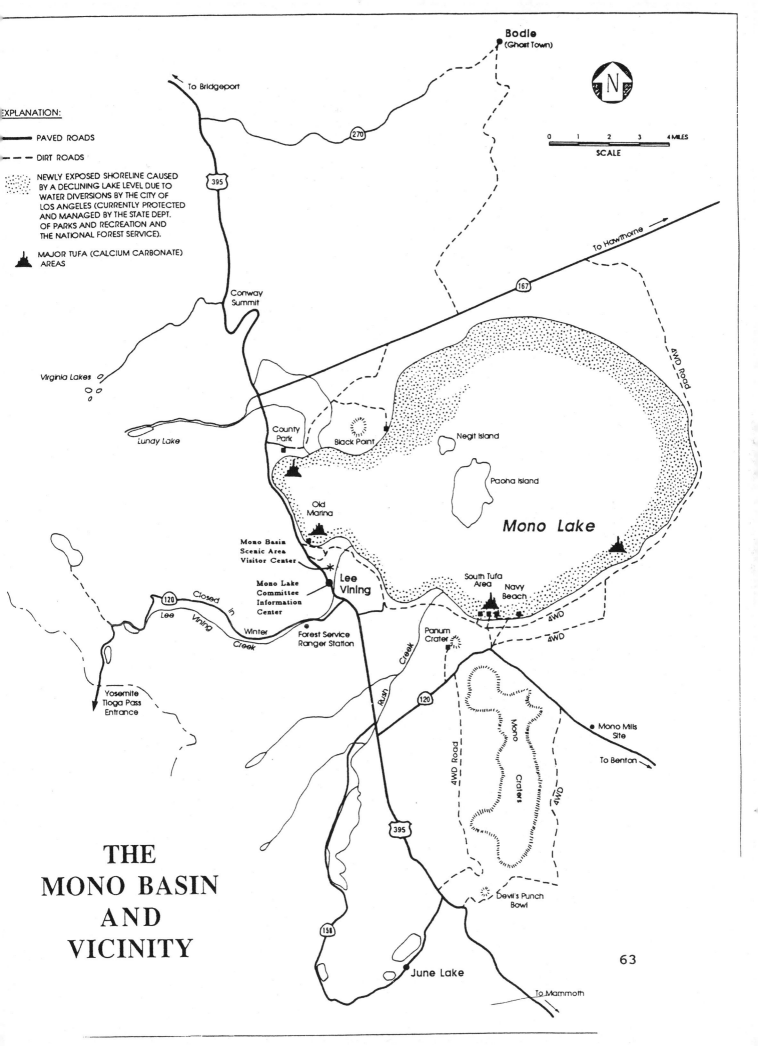

EXPLANATION:

———— PAVED ROADS

----- DIRT ROADS

NEWLY EXPOSED SHORELINE CAUSED BY A DECLINING LAKE LEVEL DUE TO WATER DIVERSIONS BY THE CITY OF LOS ANGELES (CURRENTLY PROTECTED AND MANAGED BY THE STATE DEPT. OF PARKS AND RECREATION AND THE NATIONAL FOREST SERVICE).

MAJOR TUFA (CALCIUM CARBONATE) AREAS

To Bridgeport

Bodie (Ghost Town)

N

0 1 2 3 4 MILES
SCALE

To Hawthorne

270

395

Conway Summit

167

4WD Road

Virginia Lakes

Lundy Lake

County Park

Black Point

Negit Island

Paoha Island

Mono Lake

Old Marina

Mono Basin Scenic Area Visitor Center

Mono Lake Committee Information Center

Lee Vining

South Tufa Area

Navy Beach

120 Closed In

Lee Vining Creek

Winter

Forest Service Ranger Station

4WD

4WD

Panum Crater

Yosemite Tioga Pass Entrance

Rush Creek

120

4WD Road

Mono Craters

4WD

Mono Mills Site

To Benton

395

Devil's Punch Bowl

THE
MONO BASIN
AND
VICINITY

158

June Lake

63

To Mammoth

Return to the main highway and proceed south a few miles towards LeeVining, where you will see, on the left, a strange looking new building on a bluff overlooking the lake. This is the new Mono Basin Scenic Area Visitors Center and it is well worth a hour or so visit. There is ample parking, and there is no admittance fee. This Center offers hands-on exhibits, two art galleries showcasing local artists and the famous "At Mono Lake" photographic exhibit, a 95 seat theater showing the film "Of Ice and Fire", a portrait of the Mono Basin and the Eastern Sierra Interpretive Association Bookstore. It is all most tastefully done and most instructive. Do not miss it.

Mono Lake is a strange, almost eerie place with a certain prehistoric quality about it. The Visitor Center can provide all the information you desire and the book store is replete with volumes concerning this area.

In 1854 Leroy Vining established a "location" in Vining's Gulch, a steep ravine to the west of Mono Lake, and immediately south of the present town. Since space was restricted there, in time a small "town" began on the bluff. There are a number of motels here (it is the eastern gateway to Yosemite over the Tioga Grade, just south of town) including a Best Western. These tend to fill up early since this is a sort of mid-point between the L.A. area and the Lake Tahoe-Reno area; reservations would be desirable. There is a good restaurant four miles north -the Mono Inn- and several other eating places in town.

Vining was apparently an active person in the eastern Sierra for some time but he came to a strange end. It seems it was the custom for a boisterous crowd of miners and gamblers to congregate at the Exchange Saloon in Aurora. Being "boisterous" these frequently resulted in shooting affrays. On these occasions everyone would scramble to exit the scene. On one such occasion when a gun went off in the crowd everyone left- including Lee Vining. Shortly thereafter they found him dead on the sidewalk. Apparently a pistol had discharged in his pocket, shooting him in the groin and he bled to death.

On the following morning, after breakfasting and gassing, continue south on US 395 for 4 miles to a turnoff road to the left. This is California SR 120 and it winds through some beautiful back country including The Mono Craters area, what is left of the Mono Mills (and its forest), and to Benton Hot Springs and later Benton Station, at the intersection with US 6. See the map on the following page.

64

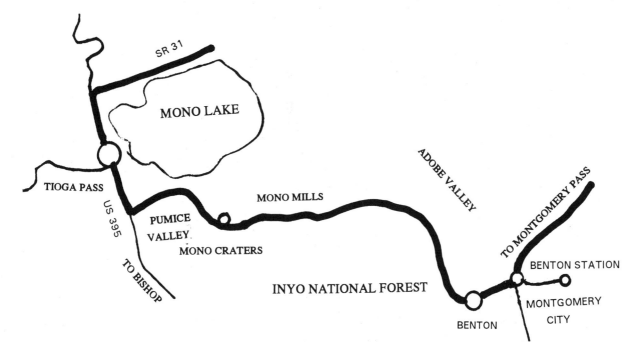

SR 120 is comparatively little known, even though it is
fully paved for the entire distance. First it crosses
Pumice Valley. This is all pumice country, and it is very
easy to bog down; stay on the roads unless you have a four
wheel drive vehicle. Most of this originated in the Mono
Craters, which stand in a row to the right. These craters
are obsidian domes, but once threw pumice (ash) for as much
as 30 miles. On the east side of these craters the ash is
still 20 feet deep. There is a side road to the Panum
Crater and several others to other craters but be careful,
stay in the packed down tire tracks at all times. Panum
Crater is a rhyolitic volcano which is 75% silica, the raw
material of glass. It is one of the youngest volcanoes in
the Eastern Sierra, erupting only about 600 years ago. A
complete investigation will take about 12 hours.

One of California's
newest State Parks,
the Mono Lake Tufa
State Reserve, em-
bodies 57,000 acres
of lakeshore and lake.
The best spots to
visit are South Tufa
and the County Park.
Check with the Infor-
mation Center for more
details.

The Inyo National Forest has installed a historical marker at the site of Mono Mills (which at one time had a general store, two boarding houses and six single residences; nothing is left at all now). The nearby town of Bodie was hungry for wood in order to build houses, provide fuel and shore up the mines. At first, wagons hauled wood from the Mono Forest to Bodie, but later the Bodie and Benton Railroad was started (in 1881) and successfully operated for nearly 50 years. It was built by Chinese labor, which caused some great resentment among white workers, and met many engineering obstacles including steep grades, deep cuts and a 260 ft trestle (50 feet high). It was abandoned in 1917. The road continues on through some high country, with great views in all directions. Eventually it reaches Benton Hot Springs. Silver was discovered near here (at Blind Springs Hill) in March 1865 and in a watered, grassy flat some two miles northwest the camp of Benton was developed.

BENTON

In less than a year it had a post office, and became a supply center for a large surrounding area. In the late 1860's a mill was erected for both local ores and those from nearby strikes, as well as a brewery -which proved to be very popular in the area. The price of silver plummeted in 1873 and most of the mines closed. Early in the 1880's the Bodie and Benton Railroad was projected to reach this place and grading commenced, but it stopped short -at Black Lake- about 5 miles to the west. It is still a rich farming and fruit growing area and one where vineyards are said to flourish.

Continue on 4 miles to Benton Station. This is now mostly a place name, although in earlier days it was a connection point to US6 - the road that goes south into Bishop. Due east of this point a few miles up a steep canyon in the

White Mountains is the forgotten town of Montgomery, California. Rich silver veins were discovered here in 1863 and a District was formed. The camp was always small but had a newspaper (the Pioneer). No further worthwhile veins were found and the camp soon folded.

Turn north (left) here and then travel 6 miles to the Nevada-California State line, then 8.4 miles through Queen Valley (the White Mountains with Boundary Peak, the highest point at 13,143 feet are on the right) to Montgomery Pass. Sopers Hotel and Casino (formerly the Montgomery Lodge/Casino) is located here and it is a convenient place for a "pitstop" and perhaps a cold drink. The Carson and Colorado Railroad, serving the former towns of Belleville, Candelaria and Marietta went though this pass; if you look closely, you may be able to trace part of the roadbed but much of it is now the highway. Continue east on US 6 to the cutoff road to US 395 which extends 26 miles through the totally deserted site of Belleville to an intersection with US 395 at Rhodes Salt Marsh. Salt pools were discovered here in 1862 when it was called the Virginia Salt Marsh. Imported camels transported the salt to the mills near Virginia City. By 1881 the marsh has been worked extensively for both salt and borax. Borax mining continued and in 1882 Rhodes became a station on the Carson and Colorado Railroad. Some mining continued until 1911. North on this main highway a few miles you will see a dirt road to the left marked "Candelaria." It was first prospected in 1863, but it was not until later, when the Northern Belle Mine began, that it became successful. In 1876 there was a two block business district, but water was extremely limited, being brought from Columbus by pack train at $1.50 per small barrel. This was when the average daily miner's wage was about $4.00. In 1880 there were 900 people, but almost twice that three years later. Much of this growth reflected the construction of the Carson and Colorado Railroad which reached the town in 1882, but it also related to the development of a dependable water system. Then there were 27 saloons (none depending on water) but no churches. By the 1890's the town was noticeably declining. In 1979 some mining resumed and even today there is some activity. There is no shade here and no water, but it is an interesting short side trip and probably will be the only time that you will ever visit the place. Continue past the towns of Mina, Luning, Hawthorne, and then along the west shore of Walker Lake to a cluster of trees and a few buildings. This is the site of Dutch Creek. An old Dutchman first opened a mine here in the summer of 1867, but the area was subsequently closed when the Federal Government started the Ammunition Depot. In 1906 the "Feds" opened this part of the reservation for exploration and several hundred miners, speculators and prospectors rushed into the area- most headed for the Dutchman Mine. Overnight a camp developed (it was a very wild place). There were always great expectations but little production. It virtually died in 1907 and little was left by 1909. Continue on to Schurz (an Indian colony and settlement). Veer west at the fork here on the road to Yerington. Three and a half miles west and south of Schurz, back in the hills to the south, is the long forgotten town of Granite. Gold was discovered here, at the north end of the Wassuk Range, in the spring of 1908 and a District was duly formed. The town soon supported a post office, a hand written newspaper and some stores. The boom subsided as quickly as it began however, and by 1912 it was all over, although a few mines continued until 1916. Continue through Yerington and then north (on Alt 95) which leads to Silver Springs. Carsonites turn off here west on US 50 while those heading to Reno/Sparks continue north to Fernley, where I-80 returns to the point of beginning.

6 Carson City to Minden/Gardnerville, Woodfords, Markleeville, Silver Mountain, Ebbets Pass, Lake Alpine, Bear Valley, Arnold, Murphys, Sonora (overnight), Jamestown, Twain Harte, Sonora Pass, Pickle Meadows, Walker, Topaz and return.

As usual this trip commences in Carson City (or Reno/Sparks as the case may be), and returns there. The trip out -over Ebbets Pass to Sonora- (the overnight stop) is about 145 miles and requires about 3-1/2 hours of driving time; the return trip over Sonora Pass, is also about 145 miles and is also 3-1/2 hours of driving time. In both cases, however, these are minimums; extra time should be allotted for "wandering, shopping and looking".

Head south on US 395 to the "Y" just outside of Minden, where it intersects SR 88; The Carson Pass road. Continue south on SR 88 until Woodfords, where SR 89 (and SR4) intersect. This place was known earlier as Carey's Mill, and even before that as Brannan's Springs. Turn left here, passing a county campground at Turtle Rock and the road to Indian Creek campground, some 6 miles to Markleeville. Jacob Marklee was the first resident here, taking up 160 acres in September 1859. He built a cabin on what is now the site of the Court House and operated a toll bridge across Markleevillle Creek. In the Spring of 1863 he was found murdered on the front stoop of his cabin. In 1865 there were 1660 people in the newly formed Alpine County; this decreased to 172 by 1875 and is now about 1600.

It is worth a moment to stop here and look around, especially in two places: the Alpine Hotel- the site of the famous Cutthroat Saloon, and the Markleeville General Store- which is exactly that, one of a dying breed. The Alpine Hotel was originally the famous Fisk Hotel in Silver Mountain City. It was taken apart in sections, moved to Markleeville and renamed the Hot Springs Hotel. Later, it was again renamed- to the Alpine Hotel.

Continue on this road across the bridge (Markleeville Creek) to Hangman's Bridge over the East Fork of the Carson River. Continue along the river to the intersection of SR 89- The Monitor Pass road. At this point the main road becomes SR 4 and continues, past the Scossa cowcamp, (the very rugged rocks on the right is the site of the famous IXL mine), to the Silver Mountain City campground and monument. Silver Mountain City, at first named Kongsberg after a Norwegian silver mining town, was active from 1860 to 1880. It reached a peak population of 3,120, but today little remains except a few stone foundations. It became the County Seat in 1864 when Alpine County was created, but

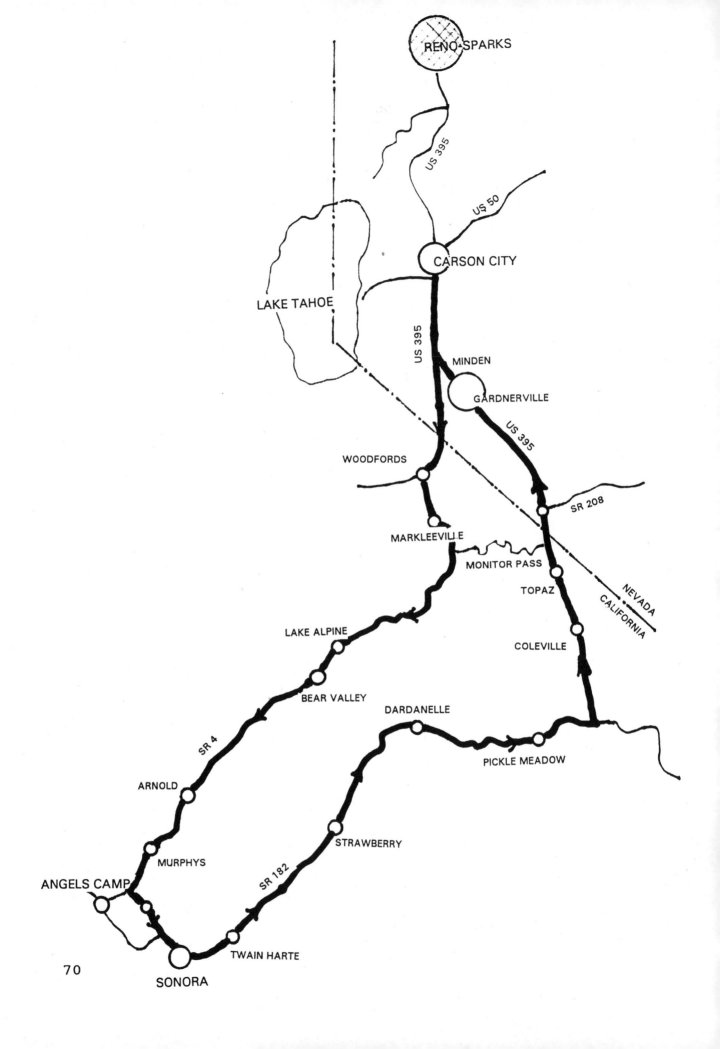

RENO-SPARKS

US 395

US 50

CARSON CITY

LAKE TAHOE

US 395

MINDEN

GARDNERVILLE

US 395

WOODFORDS

SR 208

MARKLEEVILLE

MONITOR PASS

TOPAZ

NEVADA

CALIFORNIA

LAKE ALPINE

COLEVILLE

BEAR VALLEY

DARDANELLE

SR 4

PICKLE MEADOW

ARNOLD

STRAWBERRY

MURPHYS

ANGELS CAMP

SR 182

TWAIN HARTE

70

SONORA

the population dwindled to only 200 by 1868 and the County Seat was moved to Markleeville. Continuing, pass a snowgate at the 7,000 foot elevation, and then up a steep and twisting road to Kinney Lake, just short of the summit. This is a very pretty, clear blue lake which is always popular with fishermen. Ebbets Pass Summit (8730 feet) is quite near; this is where the Pacific Crest Trail- from Mexico to Canada- crosses the highway. The Pass was named for Major John Ebbets, who crossed here in April 1850. Black Knob, a very descriptive name for this mountain, is on the right. Go on down the west side to Hermit Valley, a very old stopping place first known as Holden's in the early 1860's -There is a sign there- see the picture below.

Mosquito Lakes are a short distance more. There are consistently great views all along here of the really high country of the Sierra. Lake Alpine at the 7,000 foot altitude is next, with numerous campsites as well as gas and supplies. It was formed in 1862 when a dam was built across Silver Creek, a tributary of the Stanislaus River. The Mt. Reba Ski Resort is a short distance west. A few more miles is Bear Valley (56 miles, 1-1/2 hours from Minden) which was originally called "Grizzly Bear Valley". A Harvey Blood, who once owned the Sperry and Perry Hotel in Murphys, married Elizabeth Gardner (Dorrington) and had one daughter- Reba. He was an early settler in Bear Valley, taking up a land patent for its use as a summer stock range. He established the main toll gate for the Big Trees-Carson Valley turnpike in 1862, which he owned and operated for many years. He was a dedicated Mason and would often ride horseback from Bear Valley some 40 miles down the mountain to Angels Camp, attend the Lodge meeting, and then ride back the next day. During the last ten years or so Bear Valley has become a veritable "city" for the region. Lodging, gas, restaurants, a general store, art galleries and extensive skiing are available here.

The road continues down the mountain, through Tamarack (known originally as Onion Valley for the many wild onions there), Big Meadows and then Cottage Springs (now a subdivision, summer mountain cabins area and winter ski resort) to Dorrington. The old hotel here was built in 1860 by John and Rebecca Gardner and was a stagecoach stop on the Big Trees-Carson Valley toll road from 1862 to 1910. It was also a depot for stockmen and operated as a summer resort. It is the site of an ice-cold spring. It was originally known as Cold Spring Ranch, until the post office was started in 1902, when it became known as Dorrington's. The hotel has been restored with five elegant rooms fitted with Victorian antiques. The dining room serves exceptional (northern Italian) dinners: no children or pets. (Call 209-795-5800 for information). The Washoe Indians from the Walker River country in Nevada would come here for their summer encampments. A few Paiutes came too, bringing pine nuts and woven baskets to sell or trade.

DORRINGTON (HOTEL)

Just around the corner is the Calaveras Big Trees State Park. This is the site of numerous giant Sierra Redwoods (Sequoia Gigantea) as well as extensive stands of mixed conifers, Mountain Dogwood and White Alder. There are a number of identified walking trails, which can take from 1-1/2 hour to 3 hours (or more). There is a small admission fee; seniors are $4.00/vehicle.

72

CALAVERAS BIG TREES

Eight miles further is the booming town of Arnold which is rapidly developing as a retirement community since it is below the snow line but above the valley heat and fog. There is a golf course here: the Meadowwood- for those interested. Twelve miles further is Murphys, a most charming old gold town first known as "Murphys Rich Diggins" and later "Murphys Camp". It is now just plain Murphys. It was the western terminus of the Emigrant Road across the Sierra and was also the destination of Snowshoe Thompson on his famous 90 mile mail trek across the mountains from Carson Valley to the west side. John and Dan Murphy, two Irish brothers, discovered gold here in 1848. John then established a trading post to furnish supplies to the MiWuk Indians whom he had persuaded to wash gravel for him. He offered fair treatment to these Indians and, in fact, married the daughter of the local Chief. After only a year of operations, it is said that he left camp with 17 mules loaded with gold of an estimated value of 1.75 million dollars (1850 dollars!). It is known that Wells Fargo and Co. shipped 15 million dollars worth of gold dust from Murphys during a ten year period extending from the 1850's to the '60's.

HOTEL IN MURPHYS

Five miles further, at Vallecito, the Murphy brothers also discovered gold in 1848. Turn left on Cal 18-E through rolling hills where there are a number of small developing wineries. Many offer "tasting experiences". You will soon see the signs for the " Moaning Cavern". This is a single large gallery (large enough to stand the entire Statue of Liberty in it) which also contains the oldest human remains yet found in America. There is a giant 14 foot long stalactite and huge stalagmites as well. There is a 100 foot spiral staircase which descends into this cavern but the more adventuresome can utilize a rappel - a 180 foot rope descent - "mountaineering style" into the deeper, undeveloped and unlighted areas, using lighted helmets, ropes and professional guides. As their brochure states: "we supply the coveralls, gloves, hardhats and the highest quality equipment available; you supply the courage." Call 209-736-2708 for details.

Leaving here, cross the river to Columbia State Historic Park, a preserved and reconstructed monument to the way it was. George and Thaddeus Hildreth, two brothers from Maine, came to San Francisco in 1849, joined with three new friends and all headed for the Sierra to make their fortunes. At Woods Crossing, near Jamestown they began, but soon "saw the elephant" (mining was hard work) and not nearly as remunerative as they had heard. The five wandered around the area a bit and finally on March 27, 1850, struck pay dirt in Kennebec Hill (obviously a Maine name), afterwards called "Hildreths's Diggin's." The first miners were realizing two pounds of gold per day, but that soon diminished to only one pound per day. News of this spread rapidly and a month later the population of the camp was about 6,000 (it finally reached 15,000). Brush ramadas and canvas tents flourished and were sprinkled everywhere. Saloons and gambling quickly followed (in the first few weeks, 143 Monte Banks were in operation with a combined capital of about one million dollars). It was a brawling, wild camp, especially during its infancy. On June 1850 a" Foreign Miners Tax" went into effect in California; it was intended to force Mexicans, South Americans and Chinese miners off of their claims- which it did. Many of these turned to gambling and banditry (Joaquin Murieta of this area, was the most famous). That June, 12 murders took place here in a single week. In July, 1854 most of the town was destroyed by fire and in August, 1857 this was repeated. The Comstock strike in 1859 lured many of the Columbia population to Virginia City (Nevada). In 1945 the State of California purchased the main business district to create the Historical Park and one by one the buildings were reconstituted. There are many things to see and to do. Admission is free. There are guided tours, gold panning, stagecoach rides, museums, a visit to an Assay office, shopping, live theater (at the Fallon House), several 1850 saloons and old buildings to poke around (and into). It could take a long time, depending on your interests.

FALLON THEATRE - COLUMBIA

It is then only a few miles on into Sonora. Originally established as two adjoining mining towns, called "Sonoranian Camp" and "Camp Americano", both operated by Mexicans from Sonora (Mexico). In 1848 they became one and were soon known as the "Queen of the Southern Mines". No one knows for sure but it is thought that about $40 million in gold was taken from the surrounding hills. The large nugget- The Golden Chispas- weighing over 28 pounds was found here. In 1850 it became the County Seat, which it still is, as well as the hub of most County activity. There are many excellent examples of Victorian homes scattered around, and the community is designated as one of only 5 "California Main Street Cities". The many shops are elegant with a variety of stores, jewelers, boutiques, galleries and restaurants. Do not miss the County Museum, formerly the County jail which was built in 1857. There are a wide variety of accommodations, from hotels to B&B's; additional lodgings are to be found in nearby Jamestown. There is also a golf course here; Mountain Springs, an 18 hole Robert Graves design. There is a pro shop, a club house and a dining room. It is located on Lime Kiln Road (call 209-532-1000). There is also a Visitors Bureau in town which is very knowledgeable and helpful.

A side trip will take you a few miles (west on SR 108) to Jamestown- the self proclaimed "Gateway to the Mother Lode". Gold was first discovered in Tuolumne County ("Tuolumne is a MiWuk Indian name which means "Stone House") between Jamestown and Sonora in 1848. This drew hundreds of miners, including one "Col." George James, a lawyer from San Francisco. He immediately became involved in some mining but much speculation until he and his wife disappeared one night in 1849 with all the gold he could lay his hands on. Tensions ran high, and in a fit of anger the name of the town was changed, but it eventually returned to its present name. It was first a tent-town, with plentiful bawdy houses, fandango parlors and other sin palaces, but later "improved" to include thirty saloons, five hotels and numerous stores. Today it is a tourist center, with many B&Bs, gourmet restaurants, antique shops, art galleries; even gold panning on the main street. If you arrive here at the proper time have dinner at Michelangelo- a very fine Italian restaurant on the main street. The chef is a graduate of the California Culinary Institute, and everything is done with flair and excellence. The Hotel Willow Restaurant and Saloon has an 1890 elegance (prime ribs are a specialty) and the National Hotel, built in 1859, has a turn of the Century ambience. The Bella Union, originally a restaurant and dance hall, burned in 1900 and rebuilt with an 1880's decor is complete, even with an old Brunswick Bar which was brought round the Horn in a sailing ship in 1880. Wild game and pastas are their forte.

The following morning visit the nearby California State Historic Railway Park (Railtown). This is a family experience featuring 26 acres of railroadiana, including a roundhouse, shop complex, steam locomotives and passenger cars, all which served the area since 1897. Many movies and TV series have been filmed here. Daily tours are offered year round and steam train rides are available on weekends from March to November. Call 209-984-3953.

Leaving Sonora, following a "Miner's Breakfast" (biscuits and gravy) and after topping the gas tank, follow SR 108 east miles to Twain Harte. This quaint community is nestled in pine trees at an elevation of 3800 feet. It is now a growing retirement and vacation community with neat homes, charming inns and superior dining (plus sidewalk cafes). Shops offer fine arts, clothing, local crafts and antiques. There is also a public golf course.

Return to the new highway and proceed easterly , bypassing Sugarpine (historic landmark), to Miwuk Village. The Miwuk (or Miwok) Indians, native to the area, lived here for thousands of years, trapping small game, fishing and gathering acorns, seeds and mushrooms. They did not wander much but stayed close to their home grounds. They are famous for their fine, closely woven baskets. Continue past Longbarn, to Pinecrest and then Strawberry on the South Fork of the Stanislaus River. Throughout all of this you will be amazed by the light traffic and the total absence of trucks. Pinecrest is the entry point to the Dodge Ridge Ski area.

Continue east on SR 108 through magnificent high country with verdant forests and plentiful wild flowers. Boulder Flat (Brightmans) has developed camping facilities as does Dardanelles, where there is also a post office a store, lodging, gas and a restaurant. From there it is a pleasant drive along the Middle Fork of the Stanislaus River to Kennedy Meadows (Baker Station) where there is a small store and some camp grounds. It is then a steep grade through Deadmans to Sonora Pass at 9,624 feet. There is a sign here indicating that Andrew Fletcher conceived the idea of a wagon road through this pass to connect the booming mines of Mono County (Aurora and Bodie) with Tuolomne County points, although Jedediah Smith, that early mountain man, was the first white who crossed in 1827.

Down the steeper east side involves a 15% grade (sometimes flattening out to only 12%) with many switchbacks, but always magnificent views, especially to Leavitt Peak to the south. Soon a view of Leavitt Meadows emerges, and eventually the base of the grade is reached where there is a snow gate. Then there is a relatively mild grade of only 7% along the East Fork of the Walker River to Pickle Meadows, named for Jon Pickles, an early day rancher who was killed here in the 1880's. A Marine Corps Mountain Warfare Training Center now operates here on a 44,000 acre reserve. It was first opened in 1951 as a Cold Weather Training Station for troops bound for Korea but was expanded in 1957 to include summertime mountain training programs. It closed shortly thereafter, only to reopen in 1975 when the Viet Nam affair flared up. It has been quite active since that time. The camp now has 25 permanent personnel with a $2.2 million budget. 10,000 soldiers a year now train here, both in winter and summer high country conditions.

Continue to the US 395 intersection where there is a California State Highway Maintenance station and turn left on 395 towards Carson City- 66 miles distant. The first 18 miles parallels the river to Walker, then passes through Coleville, Topaz and on to Minden/Gardnerville.

Depending on the time, you might enjoy a stop here to: 1) the Lahontan National Fish hatchery, 2) a round of golf at the Carson Valley Country Club on Riverview Drive, and 3) a fabulous Prime Rib dinner in Gardnerville at Sharkeys, a local personage, whose " joint" is a veritable museum in its own right. Sharkey is indeed a character; he is always there, and his place is a most unique holdover in the now neon and plastic world that is modern Nevada gaming. Prime rib is his specialty and the serving laps the (large) plate on both ends.

Continue north on U.S. 395 through the northern portion of Carson Valley, over Indian Hill and into Carson City, the point of beginning.

MAIN STREET GARDNERVILLE (DATE UNKNOWN)

7 Reno/Carson to Lovelock, Oreana, Rochester, Fitting, Unionville (overnight), Mill City, Coal Canyon, Fortymile Desert, Fallon and return.

This trip is another overnighter; this one into the wilds of central Nevada; primarily to visit the well known "ghost town" of Unionville, but also to sample some of the other historic and natural attractions of the nearby area. For the most part it utilizes paved highways, although some visitations, especially out of Unionville, are on dirt roads; these are all passable and a four wheel drive (while nice) is not necessary. As is usual for all of these trips, come prepared with proper equipment and survival gear, including at least one spare tire and the tools to change it - since one never knows. The route out to Unionville totals some 130 miles and will require about 2-1/2 hours; the route back is approximately 160 miles and will require about the same time. In both cases the time involved is dependent on "interruptions", for such mundane things as lunch and wandering around old mine ruins. This is actually a variant of Trip #3, but is only one night out- and that spent in the comfort of a B & B (if that is your choice)- call ahead.

This trip actually starts in Lovelock, some 90 miles to the east of the Reno-Sparks and Carson City areas. Lovelock, first known as " Big Meadows" was settled by George Lovelock in 1868, when the Central Pacific Railroad came to this place. It soon became a center for surrounding mining endeavors and a site of agricultural development. By 1900 there were about 100 houses and a suitable business district. Originally a part of Humboldt County, it was split in 1918 and renamed Pershing County, after the famous General of that time. It will take about 90 minutes to get there from all three locales since it is all freeway driving. Lovelock is not too exciting, but then it is only the I.P.(initial point) in this case and no time will be spent in seeing the sights of this metropolis.

Proceed east from Lovelock on I-80 another 14 miles to the Oreana turnoff (well signed). As usual, this turnoff to dirt roads is the "real " beginning. See the route map on the following page. Turn right here to the Limerick Canyon Road. Shortly there will be a dirt road to the right which is unsigned. This is the Rochester Canyon Road and it leads up into a box canyon in which the sites of both Upper and Lower Rochester are located: Miners from Rochester, New York, found gold here in the early '60's but nothing much was done until the summer of 1912. Then there was a wild rush which continued into the winter. In 1913 some 2200 men were in the two camps along the 2-1/2 mile long main

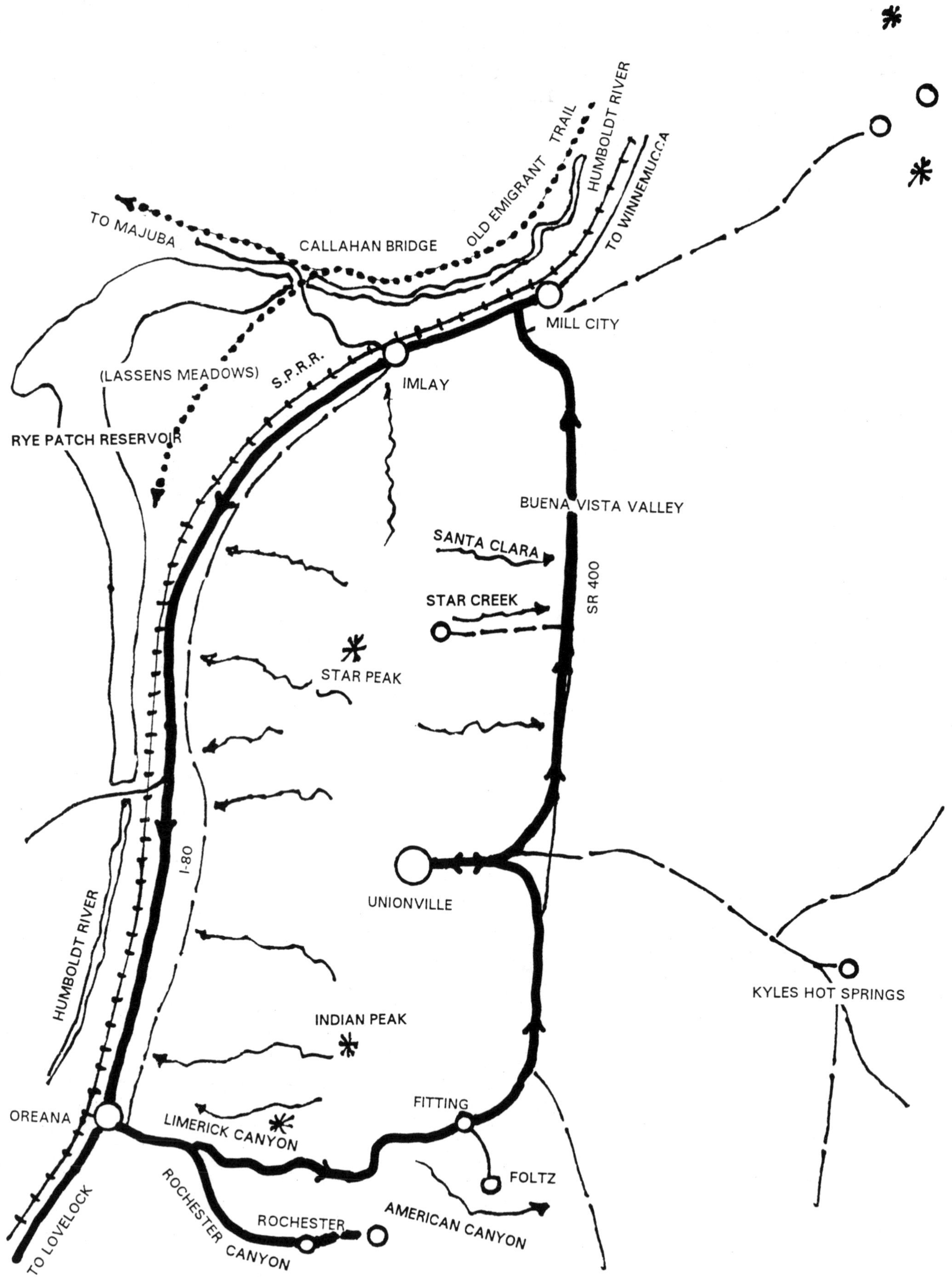

TO MAJUBA

CALLAHAN BRIDGE

OLD EMIGRANT TRAIL

HUMBOLDT RIVER

TO WINNEMUCCA

MILL CITY

(LASSENS MEADOWS)

S.P.R.R.

IMLAY

RYE PATCH RESERVOIR

BUENA VISTA VALLEY

SANTA CLARA

STAR CREEK

SR 400

STAR PEAK

HUMBOLDT RIVER

I-80

UNIONVILLE

KYLES HOT SPRINGS

INDIAN PEAK

OREANA

LIMERICK CANYON

FITTING

FOLTZ

ROCHESTER CANYON

ROCHESTER

AMERICAN CANYON

TO LOVELOCK

80

street from Lincoln Hill to Nenzel Hill. Saloons (more than half of the buildings in camp were saloons), dance halls, offices and all the other necessary commercial outlets were in place. In March, 1913 Rochester had a post office, the Rochester Philharmonic Orchestra and regular freight service consisting of twenty autos, two trucks and numerous mule outfits.

ROCHESTER

In 1914 the Nevada Short Line Railroad was extended into Limerick Canyon (to the north) and a new mill was begun (finished the following year). Lower Rochester by now was the largest camp. The Railroad was extended during the summer of 1915 and mining continued during the 20's and 30's, but by 1941 most operations had stopped and the camp was all but "dead".

ROCHESTER

Return down Rochester Canyon to its entry, then take a hard right on the newly paved "highway" up Limerick Canyon. This recently improved road leads to the Couer-Rochester mining operation which has all but leveled the whole ridge behind Upper Rochester. That site is, in fact, blocked off from access due to this extensive mining operation. This company has been mining here a number of years and currently is extracting some 65,000 ounces of gold and 5.9 million ounces of silver per year, utilizing 300 employees, most of whom live in Lovelock.

Almost to the top there once was a turnoff road to the right which went to the long abandoned site of Panama, originally a tent city of about 50 people. Started in 1913, It lasted less than a year. Then, over a low pass to American Canyon. Chinese began placering here in 1884, 3 years after a white group gave up in disgust. It was reported that as many as 3000 of them washed gravel during its peak period. Following the completion of the Central Pacific Railroad across Nevada in 1869, thousands of Chinese workers were simply "let go" to fend for themselves as best they could. Many wandered into nearby, usually remote, mining areas where they worked as menials, woodcutters, charcoal burners and truck gardeners. As a result, a large settlement developed, most of it built of native rock. There was much gambling and some opium use, but little else. It all stopped by 1895, but by then between 5 and 10 million dollars (1895 dollars that is) in gold had been removed (there is no clear record since the Chinese were somewhat secretive about that sort of thing). It was known, however, as the largest placer output in the state. This road has been blocked by mining operations and is not traversable.

From here the road goes over Spring Garden Pass and down Spring Creek to where it emerges into Buena Vista Valley. At the mouth of this canyon once was the town of Spring Valley, or Fitting (or sometime Foltz, although this was actually a camp about 3 miles to the south, named after its owner). Whatever the name, this also was a major placer area. The Chinese were here first, coming in 1881, but it was a small operation and languished until 1905, when a post office (named" Fitting") was established. Things picked up considerably, and by 1911 a 2000 yard dredge was washing gravel in a large pond in the lower ravine below the camp. A 15 stamp and amalgamating mill was also erected at that time. The population finally reached about 150 and there was even a semiweekly stage to Lovelock (which cost $3). It was a fairly active camp for the time. The most prominent lode was the Bonanza King. However ore eventually proved to be inadequate. In 1915 the post office was closed and the camp was abandoned. More recently, a Louisiana firm took over the area, did extensive grading and wrecked all of the old buildings remaining, installed new water lines, and then left, as abruptly as they came. Nothing remains today to mark even its (ephemeral) existence, except for some tailing ponds. Fitting was the long time home of Jack Omar, an original character; his story is told in my book "Travels in the Nevada Outback 1954-1992." Silver State Printing, Minden.

FITTING - ABOUT 1965

Turn north on SR 50 into Buena Vista Valley going about 16 miles to the clearly defined turnoff into Unionville Canyon. In the spring of 1861, Indians brought rich ore from Buena Vista Canyon to Virginia City. Two Comstock miners were sufficiently impressed and immediately crossed the desert with the Indian guides, arriving in May. Ten days later the District was formed and a townsite created in the upper canyon. It was at first (briefly) called Dixie- until political forces prevailed and it was renamed Unionville. In November 1861 it became the County Seat of Humboldt County. In 1862 a rival townsite developed in the lower part of the canyon which boasted 200 houses within the year. By the summer of '63' there were 1000 residents here and it had become a major distribution point for supplies shipped from California. The town included 10 stores, an express station, a brewery, an assayer, a jeweler, notaries, lawyers and even a lively weekly newspaper. Most of the camp was adobe, since lumber was scarce and what there was of it, was of very poor quality. The District peaked in 1864, declining steadily thereafter. In the early 1870's there were still three 10 stamp mills operating, all treating low grade ore from surrounding mines. A fire in 1872 and the continuing general mining slump resulted in the transfer of the County Seat to Winnemucca in the Spring of 1873. By 1880 there were only 200 inhabitants. At the head of this canyon are the remnants of several old mining operations; it requires a short walk.

This is the overnight stop. There is an operating B & B here-the Old Pioneer Garden, utilizing an old wooden home left over from the glory days. It has two bedrooms but there is another separate house with six bedrooms. Reservations are suggested; call 702-538-7585. There are no services of any kind in Unionville (except power and telephone) and no fishing is allowed in the creek through the town. There is also an excellent campground, maintained by Pershing County, at the head of the canyon. This fenced grassy area is well shaded by tall Lombardy poplars; there are tables and fire pits, even a campfire ring and an outhouse.

The following morning, if you are so inclined, it is a short drive across the valley to Kyles Hot Springs. These are somewhat decrepit, (I have heard recently that they are "trashed") but serviceable and have long been used by local people to cure "what ails them". It is rather pleasant to lounge in these hot pools and observe, unhindered, the majesty of the country- (there is plenty of it).

Return to the main valley road, proceeding north past Star Creek located in Star Canyon about 4 miles to the west. Silver was found here in 1861; by the following year the place was booming. Two years later there were 1200 residents and it was the county's largest town. It boasted two hotels, many saloons, stores, a Wells-Fargo office, stables and a post office, a school and a telegraph office. At the mouth of the canyon the Sheba Co. erected a 10 stamp mill. The town peaked in 1864-65 when seven large mining companies were in operation. The ore ran out in 1868, the stamp mill was shut down (it was moved to Unionville) and by 1871 only about 80 people were left. By 1880 it was totally deserted.

And continue on to Santa Clara Canyon. The town of Santa Clara occupied the head of this narrow gorge on the east flank of the Humboldt Range. It was formed in 1862 as a result of a silver strike. By 1864 there were over 200 crude rock dwellings (no wood was available at any price) and there was a daily mail run from Star City. It was always an active camp with strong (but often ribald) entertainments. By 1866, it had all but disappeared, and today only a few stone foundations remain. The road to it is now impassable.

Somewhere along about here originally there was a dirt road leading northeasterly towards Dun Glen that went by a "place" once called Jacob's Well, essentially a "water and whisky stop" on the Star City-Dun Glen Road during the 1860's. Its only product was high priced water and beer. A prominent sign then stated "travelers are not obliged to patronize our bar, but if they don't they are not our guests and people who are not our guests must pay one bit (12-1/2 cents) for each of the animals they water here". Then on to Dun Glen (canyon) and the earlier communities of Dun Glen and Chafey. Dun Glen started in 1862 and within a year had 250 people. A mill was erected in 1863, soon followed by hotels, stores, a post office, a school and several meetinghouses. A company of soldiers was garrisoned here from 1863 to 1865 since there was Indian trouble in the area during that period. A 10 stamp mill was built in 1867, but by 1880 only 50 people were left. Chinese placer miners came in the '80's, but by 1894 both mining and ranching was negligible. In the summer of 1908 the camp of Chafey was established (actually over the older site) and it soon had over 1000 inhabitants. It also included a post office, schools, stores, etc, but by 1913 it too was gone. This road has gone, as has Jacob's Well, as well as Dun Glen and Chafey. It is not worth the time or effort to seek out these sites.

Continue on the Buena Vista Road north to Mill City which is on I-80 and where a new modern truck depot/stop offers food, help, lodging, gasoline and entertainment, if you should need any (or all) of this. Turn left here, on the freeway, proceeding past Imlay, Rye Patch, Oreana and finally back into Lovelock.

Rather than returning to Reno on the freeway, (which is faster but always dull) you may, if you wish, opt for a little known desert road either out of Lovelock or using the Coal Canyon Road just east of that town, to a fifty (plus) mile arid circuit of the eastern side of the "forty mile desert", along the base of the Stillwater Range. If so, go south from Lovelock on Meridian Road crossing what is left of the Humboldt River. On the bank is a segment of the old California Trail which is still discernible. The road then crosses a low pass in the West Humboldt Range and down the far side to the northwestern corner of the "forty mile desert", now called the Carson Sink. Turn left along the base of the mountains for a thirty mile very dreary, dry and uninteresting connection to an intersection with the Coal Canyon Road. It is much easier to use this road to this point, avoiding the Lovelock maze completely. If you should do so, about 3 miles from the turnoff from the Freeway there will be a road to the left which goes to Willard. Gold was discovered here in 1915 which sparked a small boom and a camp of all tents. It was named after the boxer who defeated Jack Johnson (a major event of the day).

It finally enticed several hundred people and a mill was erected nearby. Another mill was constructed in 1921, but the District was never a real producer and it eventually died a slow death.

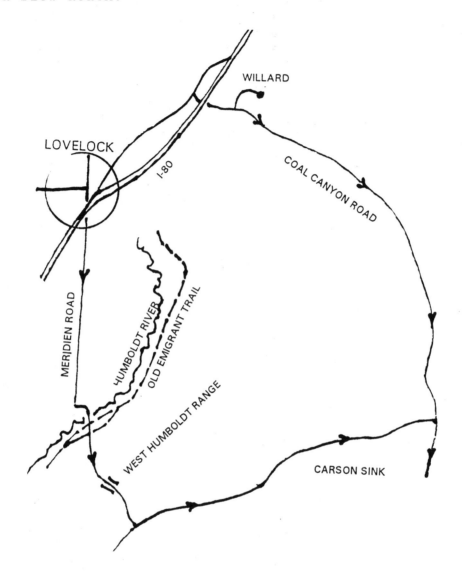

Then turn south. This is where the waters of the Carson River (formerly) fanned out and dried in the broad alkali flats north of Fallon. In the 1850's this was the most dreaded stretch on the entire Emigrant Trail and many surviving diaries reported miles of rotting carcasses, discarded belongings and wrecked wagons, which lined the entire route from the Big Meadows (Lovelock) to Ragtown on the Carson River. A more deserted and isolated region is hard to find, even today, in Nevada. The road is dirt, but hard and drivable. It follows the base of the Stillwater Range, passing a Tenneco mining operation at Fondaway Canyon, an excellent view of the terraced lake levels of ancient Lake

Lahontan, the signed road to La Plata (once the County Seat) and a "loop tour" of the Stillwater National Wildlife Refuge. Eventually it leads to the little and now mostly abandoned town of Stillwater, about 15 miles from Fallon and also once a County Seat of Churchill County as well as a station on the Overland Stage route. And then on into Fallon. The stark contrast of the last ten miles of fertile, verdant alfalfa fields here to the previous forty miles of barren desert is quite striking and somehow symbolic of the very nature of Nevada.

From here it is an easy jaunt (on paving) either through Silver Springs to Carson City or on to Fernly and then west on I-80 to the Reno-Sparks area. In either case, you may wish to stop for a moment at Ragtown, at the west end of Fallon, to read the inscription on the monument there. This was the terminus of the "40 mile" and the first fresh water. The emigrants took advantage of this to wash their now filthy garments and spread them out on the scrub trees and sagebrush (hence the name Ragtown).

8

Reno-Sparks to Susanville, Adin, Bieber, Fall River Mills (overnight), Lassen National Volcanic Park, Chester, Lake Almanor, Quincy, Blairsden, Sierraville, Truckee and return.

This overnight trip, as are all the others, begins and ends in Reno/Sparks with a turnaround point at Fall River Mills (California). The trip covers a large section of the northeastern California mountain country in Lassen, Modoc and Plumas Counties, as well as a portion of Sierra County, all of which are little known, especially by Nevadans. The trip "out" totals about 310 miles and can be driven in about six hours. The return trip is 170 miles requiring about four hours of driving time. Budget additional time, of course, to sample the little towns, have lunch and otherwise see the sights. All roads are paved and services are intermittently available, mostly in the small towns along the way. (Some, if not most, auto repair services may be closed on Sundays). See the route map below;

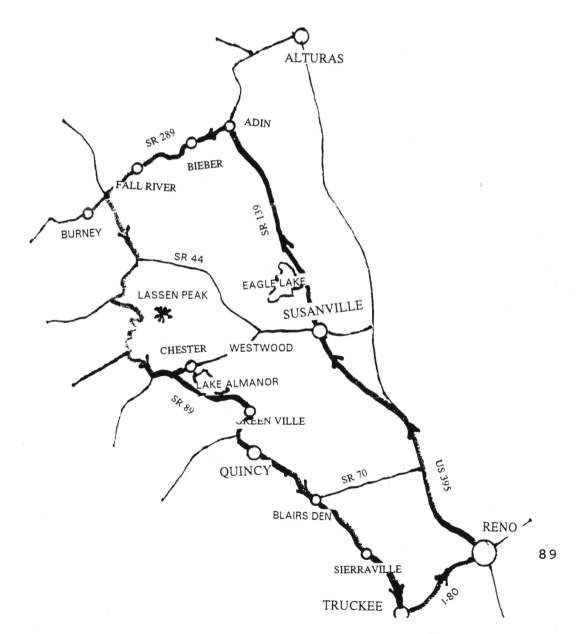

Begin by proceeding north on US 395 past Lemmon Valley, Bordertown and Hallelujah Junction into the Honey Lake Valley area. You will first pass the intersection that leads to Herlong. This site was occupied from 1892, but did not really mature until 1942, when it became the Army Ordinance Depot. Soon thereafter is the small town of Milford. First settled by Robert Scott in May of 1846, the first flour mill was erected in 1861, which was shortly followed by a grist mill and a sawmill (hence the name). A general store was opened in 1862 and soon a blacksmith also began operations. In 1864 a two story hotel and saloon as well as a post office began. In 1882 there were still three mills, a hotel, store, blacksmith, a butcher, a post office and a schoolhouse. Little remains today.

The next little town is Janesville which began with a two story log house in 1856. A blacksmith soon followed. It was originally known as Bankhead but was later changed to Janesville after Jane Bankhead, a daughter of an early settler. Due to the recurrent Indian troubles, a log stockade 63' x 90' with walls 12' high was erected. It was called "Fort Janesville." A cabin served as the first school in the early 1860's. A two story hotel was built in 1862 and a post office started in 1864. Over the years the stockade was dismantled (for the timbers) and today very little remains.

A few miles further is another small town named Johnstonville. Originally called Toadtown, it was the location of an important bridge over the Susan River. A general store was opened here in 1858 and a year later a blacksmith set up shop. The first school started in January 1863 and a gristmill began in 1865. This community was only five miles from Susanville and that town finally overwhelmed it. See the detailed map of the Susanville area on the following page.

Continue into Susanville, the county seat of Lassen County. This is the second oldest town in the Western Great Basin. Janesville is the oldest having been established as a trading post by Isaac Roop in 1854. In 1864 Lassen County was created and Susanville won a special election for the County Seat- by one vote. In 1900 it was incorporated as a city. A few years later the railroad arrived, bringing with it various activities, notably the lumber industry. It still remains a major commercial focus for the region.

There are several older structures in town which date back to the pioneer era. These include: Roop's Fort- the original trading post erected in 1854 and the first building in Lassen County; The St. Francis Hotel, built in 1914, on

90

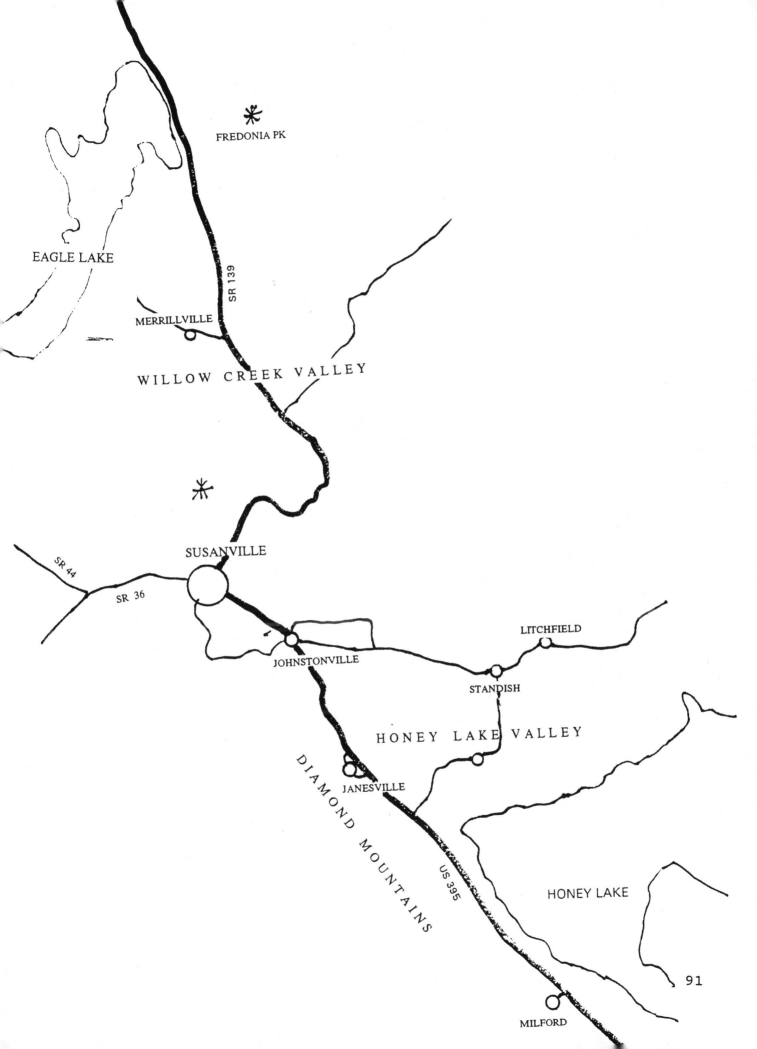

EAGLE LAKE

FREDONIA PK

SR 139

MERRILLVILLE

WILLOW CREEK VALLEY

SUSANVILLE

SR 44

SR 36

JOHNSTONVILLE

LITCHFIELD

STANDISH

HONEY LAKE VALLEY

DIAMOND MOUNTAINS

JANESVILLE

US 395

HONEY LAKE

91

MILFORD

the former site of the Magnolia Hotel, which in the mid 1860's housed county governmental functions until a courthouse could be built; The Torrey Drugs building, founded in 1921, was the previous site of the Owl Saloon during the turn of the century (where Shorty Douglas, a local character, long presided at the bar); The Pioneer Saloon, which as been at its present location since 1862 and is the oldest business in northeastern California. The barber shop on the corner has been there almost as long and for many years was operated by Sam Dotson, a well known individual; The Elks building crowns the top of Main Street. Built in 1884 as a dental office and residence for Dr. J.G. Leonard, it was acquired in 1922 by the B.P.O.E. for a lodge.

Lassen County is a leader in the development of alternative energy sources. Due to its location in an area with a history of volcanic activity, the county has a readily available supply of hot ground water. In 1974 community leaders began a program to utilize available geothermal energy in order to reduce costs. Currently four wells heat 17 public buildings and 24 residences. Near Litchfield two geothermal wells pump over 1,000 g.p.m. of 180 degree water. This heats a portion of the nearby 3,700 bed State of California correctional facility. A few miles east of Litchfield, near Wendel, HI Power operates a 35 megawatt power generating unit which combines waste wood chips with geothermal water to produce steam.

Take SR 139 north out of Susanville, soon passing the 165 acre Lassen College. This two year community college has served the area since 1925. It offers general education, vocational programs, continuing education and cultural activities. There is also a nationally recognized gunsmithing program. Continue past Jack Valley (historic monument) to Willow Creek Valley. This area was first settled in 1858, but Indians were rampant at that time and it was soon abandoned only to be reborn in 1861. The "Town of Leesburg", consisting of a cluster of five cabins, was created in the upper end of the valley (near present Merrillville.) in the 1870's. A post office existed there in 1875.

Continue on to Eagle Lake, a 42 square mile lake at 5100 feet elevation. It is nationally known for its trout fishing (average size is 3-5 pounds, the largest fish of record was 15 pounds). Five national forest campgrounds are in the pines at the south end of the lake and the BLM maintains a facility at the north end. Bird watching is a popular activity here: bald eagles, pelicans and osprey are often seen as well as many other shore birds. Continue over a pass to Grasshopper Valley, which also once had a post office (in 1875). Just beyond this there is a dirt road to the west leading 4 miles to the deserted town of Hayden Hill,

which is still a gold producer. This was a very active
mining area in the early days. The highway then follows
down Willow Creek into the little town of Adin (73 miles
from Susanville). Adin is the main settlement of Big
Valley. This is also an old town, first settled in 1869 by
Adin Gainey McDowell, a settler from Kentucky. By April,
1870 there were 350 people there. A post office opened in
1871 (Aidenville Post Office) and by March of '72' the town
boasted two stores, two saloons, two blacksmiths, a hotel,
a carpenter shop, regular church services and a general
store. By 1875 this had expanded to include a livery stable, a drug store, a doctor, several saloons and even a
lawyer. By 1877 Adin was the largest town in the county,
and was growing more rapidly than any other. Early wooden
houses were being replaced by brick and a new two story
hotel and a new brick schoolhouse were under construction.
By 1878 there were three hotels, (Franks, The Adin, and The
Modoc), a brewery, a bootmaker, a planing mill, a hair-
dressing parlor and a newspaper- the Adin Hawkeye. It was
also a staging center with daily stages from Redding. Other
carriers then scattered through the far flung area to serve
a number of small remote "towns". Time has dwindled its
importance but there are still "five hundred souls, if you
include all the dogs and cats" according to the local
storekeeper.

GENERAL STORE - ADIN

Adin and Bieber lie in Big Valley, which as the name
implies, is a big valley. It is surrounded by mountain
peaks of the southern Cascade Range. High altitude alfalfa
hay is the main crop although a new more exotic crop- wild
rice- is gaining favor. Seed potatoes and Christmas trees

offer additional yields as, of course, does lumbering. Many lakes and streams offer outstanding fishing- for trout and bass in the colder streams and bass and catfish in the warmer Pit River. Many varieties of ducks and geese use this valley as a nesting spot on the migratory flyway. There are also many upland birds; bird watching, in fact, is one the more popular local sports.

Turn left here (west) on SR 299, 10 miles to Bieber. This town started in 1877 as a single cabin homestead. It is located at Chalk Ford, on the Pit River. Nathan Bieber, a very young German lad opened a general store here that year and the following year a blacksmith joined him, then a saloon. A hotel was built in 1878 and a second general store appeared in 1879, as did a two story frame Oddfellows Hall over Brownells Store. By 1880 there was a blacksmith, two shoemakers, a livery stable, a restaurant, hotel, three saloons (including the Chalkford Saloon and the OLD Chalkford Saloon), two general stores, a variety store ("stocked with a variety of fruit and toothsome articles, also good cigars and tobacco"). A year later there were two public houses and by the fall of 1880 the first school was in operation- in the town hall. Today it is a rather dreary echo of its former glory.

And then 18 miles to McArthur and 4 miles further to Fall River Mills. Neither are particularly impressive, although Fall River Mills has a hospital.

12 miles further is the intersection with to SR 89. Six miles further is the town of Burney, a somewhat larger tourist community with expanded services and accommodations. At this point turn left (south) 22 miles along scenic Hat Creek to "Old Station" where SR 44 turns off towards Sierraville. The road now becomes SR 44. Turn right, over a low pass to the north entrance to Lassen Park. Lassen Volcanic National Park is one of the wonders of California but it is not very well known, primarily due to its relative inaccessibility. The park is the world's largest Plug Dome Volcano. It developed as a volcanic vent on the north flank of the (older) Mt. Tehama, formed 600,000 years ago. This is the southernmost volcano in the Cascade Range. It last erupted in May of 1914, beginning a seven year cycle of sporadic subsequent outbursts. In 1915 it blew again producing an enormous mushroom cloud seven miles high into the sky. In 1916 it became a National Park. Extensive thermal areas are usually associated with volcanic activity. Bumpas Hell (the largest) exhibits bubbling mud pots, steaming fumaroles and boiling water. There are seven campgrounds in the park. There are also 150 miles of hiking trails, including a 17 mile section of the Pacific Crest Trail and a portion of the old Noble's Emigrant Road. The road through is paved

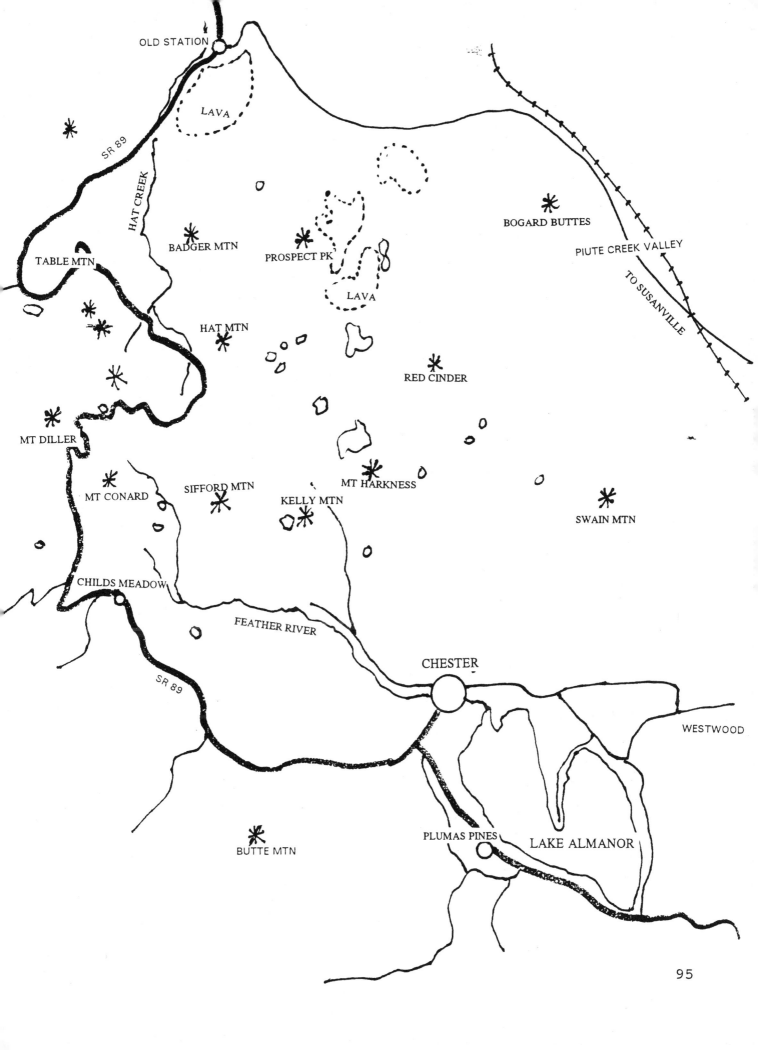

OLD STATION

LAVA

SR 89

HAT CREEK

BADGER MTN

PROSPECT PK

LAVA

BOGARD BUTTES

PIUTE CREEK VALLEY

TO SUSANVILLE

TABLE MTN

HAT MTN

RED CINDER

MT DILLER

SIFFORD MTN

MT HARKNESS

MT CONARD

KELLY MTN

SWAIN MTN

CHILDS MEADOW

FEATHER RIVER

CHESTER

WESTWOOD

SR 89

BUTTE MTN

PLUMAS PINES

LAKE ALMANOR

95

and although there are a few steep grades and some switch-backs, it is easily drivable. The road through the park is about 34 miles and will require at least an hour of driving time. Stop and inspect the many (signed) features. It is all quite unique and quite interesting.

Exit the park at the south end at the intersection of SR 36. Turn left through Mill Creek Meadows, Chiles Meadows Resort, and past the intersection with SR 32 (to Chico), and then over Deer Creek Pass towards Chester. A post office was established here in 1894 since it was a developing stage stop and dairy ranch. It was named after Chester, Missouri and Chester, Vermont, home towns of the two earliest settlers. The town began in 1909 when several subdivisions were platted. During the prohibition years it was known as "Little Reno" complete with craps, slots and poker tables, as well as a well known center for bootleggers. There are six motels in and near Chester. All are in the 10-18 units range at $30-50/day (plus tax). There are also two B & B's at $60-95$/night.

Three miles short of that small town is a turnoff on SR 89 along the west shore of Lake Almanor. Originally known as Big Meadows, this artificial lake was dammed in 1914, creating a lake 13 miles long and 6 miles wide with 52 miles of shoreline. Almanor is named for ALice, MArtha and Eli-NORe, daughters of Guy Earl, Vice President of Great Western Power Co., which later became a part of P G and E, owners of the lake's water and shoreline. This is an interesting place, quite reminiscent of Lake Tahoe 40 years ago, with rustic (summer only) cabins and a low level of activity without the neon lights and the traffic now associated with Tahoe. There are two golf courses in this area: the Lake Almanor Country Club on the peninsula is a nine hole course with a length of 2,919 yards (par 35). Open to non members after 3:00 p.m. and Lake Almanor West. Located on the west shore, this is also nine holes but with a length of 6,293 yards (18 holes), par 72.

Better, (but still old) lodging is available around the lakeshore. This includes the Almanor Lakeside Lodge and the Dorado Inn, both on the southeast shore, offering lakefront housekeeping units with full kitchens, launch ramps, (some woodstoves) at around $60-80/night. Plumas Pines Resort, about 7 miles south of Chester on the west shore, has 19 units, some with kitchens at $50-95/night. There is also a boat launch and a riding stable, as well as a nice restaurant (Fox's Lakeside Cafe) and a gift shop and grocery store. This is a good overnight stopping point.

The next morning, continue south along the lakeshore to the dam, diverting south there through Greenville. This is the commercial center and largest community in Indian Valley. In 1851 Peter Lassen found the area so attractive that he paused long enough to erect a cabin and trading post. Originally called Cache Valley, the name was changed when the Noble party passed through and were impressed by the large number of native Maidu Indians living there. The first house in Greenville was erected in 1852 by a person named Green. His log cabin soon became known as "Green's Hotel" - and eventually Greenville.

The hamlet of Crescent Mills is next: (an abandoned lumber town), and then to an intersection with SR 70. Turn left and it is then only 8 miles to Quincy, the largest town in the area and the county seat of Plumas County. It became that in 1854 when the State Legislature formed Plumas County from a portion of Butte County. It was named after Quincy, Illinois, the home town of the owner of the American Ranch Hotel (in American Valley where the town is located). This is an interesting town with many old "mountain gothic" homes scattered about.

While in Quincy, the Plumas County Museum is a must. Located at 500 Jackson St, directly behind the Court House, this facility is tastefully and completely done with a strong emphasis on an actual "living museum." It features period rooms, a country store, mining and logging memorabilia as well as an extensive array of historical publications. It is a wonderful display and well worth the (voluntary) $1.00 admission charge.

From Quincy it is 17 miles to Blairsden, the center of the Feather River Recreational area, which also includes Mohawk and Johnsville. On the way you will pass the Feather River Inn which is an old hostelry with 50 units all in the $40-50 range. Group and conference facilities, meeting rooms, catering and a golf course are available. There are, in fact, a number of golf courses in the vicinity. Besides the Feather River Inn course (nine holes, 2,744 yards, par 34) there is the Feather River Park Resort at Blairsden, nine holes, 2,582 yards, par 35; the Plumas Pines Country Club; championship 18 holes with a length of 6,504 yds, par 72, and Graeagle Meadows: a scenic 18 hole, par 72 championship course. Length: 6,688 yards.

Now there is a choice- either to turn east on SR 70, through Portola and Beckwourth to US 395 at Hallelujah Junction and then south to Reno (94 miles), or to continue on SR 89 south through Sattley and Sierraville to Truckee, and then back to Reno on I-80 (81 miles)

Presuming the latter, continue on SR 89 past the newly developing White Hawk Ranch, an upscale retirement community with an 18 hole "Championship" golf course now under construction, and on to White Sulphur Springs Ranch. This is a restored stagecoach inn with six rooms at $85-$140/night. There are also two separate cottages. Warm mineral springs and a pool are also offered. Continue to Sierraville, passing the intersection of SR 49 (the Downieville Road) and Sattley (not much). Sierraville, originally a ranch, and a general store (actually a trading post) was established in 1865. Later a post office and then a hotel, saloon and public house was added. During the '80's it became a staging center with stages running to Truckee, Loyalton, Johnstonville and Sierra City. It also developed extensive lumbering and ranching activities. As a result of this a saw and shingle mill was established, as was a door making factory. A fire in 1888 destroyed 15 buildings in the business district; only one brick building survived, which is still being used today.

Continue south on SR 89 to Truckee where there is an intercept with I-80 back to Reno. If you haven't had the opportunity to wander around "restored" Truckee, you should do so. The town is full of interesting stores, art galleries, antiques shops and the like.

9

Carson City to Minden, Carson Pass. Kirkwood,
Pioneer, West Point, Mokelumne Hill, Ione,
Plymouth (overnight), Shenandoah Valley, Amador
City, Sutter Creek, Jackson, Volcano and return.

This trip starts and ends in Carson City, with a turnaround point at Plymouth (California). The trip out totals
about 145 miles and can easily be driven in 3-1/2 hours.
The return trip is slightly shorter, at only 135 miles. A
regular passenger car is all that is required. All roads
are paved and services are readily available at frequent
intervals. The primary purpose of this overnighter is to
explore: (1) the developing vineyards of the Shenandoah
Valley of Amador County, and (2) wander though a variety of
old towns in the Sierra foothills along SR 49. These are
much better preserved than those in Nevada, are quite close
together and in general offer many more attractions and
services, even though sometimes swarming with people,
especially during the summer and fall months.

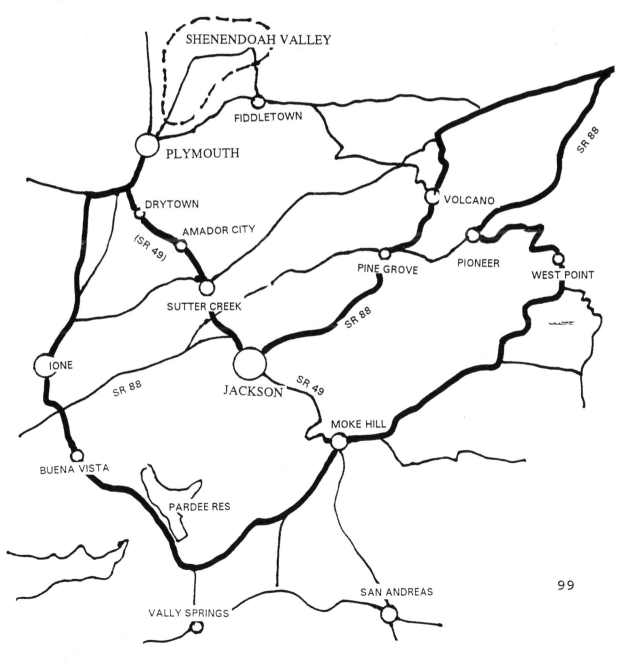

Begin by proceeding south 15 miles on U.S. 395 to the Minden "Y", then continue south on SR 88. Another 20 miles, through the south end of the green Carson Valley, is the hamlet of Woodfords. Sam Brannan, that indefatigable Mormon established a settlement here in 1847, building a cabin and some storage sheds. In 1849 Daniel Woodford built a station and in 1853 John Cary built a sawmill- also known as "Cary's Mill". By 1860 it was an important trading post and station for the Pony Express. The settlement had a mill, a saloon, a blacksmith, wagon yard, a large hotel, an unofficial post office and several residences. The inn had a painted sign featuring an elephant, which became well known in the territory. By 1867 it was a "resort" and had a dance hall with a spring floor. All was mostly destroyed by fire in 1881. The next "community is Sorenson's. Martin Sorenson came from Denmark and purchased 169 acres of land in 1916 for $750. It was first used as a base for sheep and the first cabin was erected to store supplies. A store followed, then an open air dance floor and then a gas station and finally a cafe and a few rustic cabins. In 1970 the holding was purchased by Dr. Johan Viking Hultin, a Swedish physician and cross country skier. For the following 12 years the property deteriorated and in 1982 it was sold to the Brissendens who began an immediate program to rehabilitate, adding new housekeeping cabins and restoring the buildings with an aim to create a full service destination resort. It is still far from that, but they are "getting there". A half mile further is the Luther Pass intersection in Hope Valley; the road to the right leads over Luther Pass to Lake Tahoe. Continue on SR 88 veering southerly and westerly over Carson Pass, (elev. 8573'), continuing past Caples Lake (and resort) and then on to the active Kirkwood Ski Resort. This is a fairly new activity and a short detour into the valley to look around a bit is worth the few minutes. Continuing on, SR 88 passes Silver Lake (a fishing and resort area with a small ski area), Tragedy Springs (three Mormons returning to Salt Lake City were murdered here in 1846), Maiden's Grave, Iron Mountain Ski Hill, Ham's and Cook's Stations, and the Mace Meadows area (golf course), some 77 miles to a turnoff (south) at Pioneer. This road- SR 26- leads to West Point, dipping down a steep canyon, crossing the Calaveras River, and then climbing up the other side to this town (a small retirement community of no great distinction). Two miles south is an intersection, veer right here about 6 miles to Glencoe (not much). Then another 8 miles the little town of Jesus Maria. It is then only several miles to Mokelumne Hill. This is an old and rich camp which had a wild and restless history. In October, 1848 rich deposits were found; rich enough so that sixteen square feet was considered enough for one miner's claim. This was not as unreasonable as it might sound, since some claims yielded as much as $20,000. The "Hill" was bloody; for one four month

100

period a murder a week occurred. In the good sized China-town, there were joss houses and a slave market for girls. Joaquin Murieta, the well known Mexican bandit frequented this area but was never recognized. Finally, he (at age 21) and his main lieutenant- Three Fingered Jack- were shot and killed. Moke Hill boasts the Mother Lodes first "skyscrap-er," a three story building completed in 1861 and still in good condition.

Return to SR 26 and continue westerly 3.5 miles to an intersection at which point veer right towards Paloma. This is all typical California summer hill country with dry golden grass, scattered oak trees with a few laurel, pine and cedar. Continue 4.5 miles to another intersection where again veer right, along the west edge of the Pardee Reservoir and across a one way dam road (signaled) to the Pardee Recreation Area, maintained by the East Bay Munici-pal Utility District. Soon the little town of Buena Vista in Jackson Valley appears. This is an old town with some old buildings left over from the earlier days. See the picture below of the General Store; this was moved here from Lancha Plana when Chinese miners discovered gold under the foundations.

OLD STORE - BUENA VISTA

Continue north on this road to and through the inter-section with SR 88 and then another 2 miles to Ione. Never a gold town, Ione developed as a freighting and shipping center, first to the miners, and then to the farmers and

ranchers of the area. Originally known as "Freezout" or
"Bedbug", it was the site or the Preston School of Industry
- known as the Castle- built between 1890 and 1894 as a
school for wayward juveniles. This building is no longer
occupied. This town remains (more or less) relatively intact
and has a number of old buildings still in active use. These
offer a range of antiques, gifts, food, old time bars,
various local services and browsing. There is ample parking;
most streets are well shaded and it is a pleasant place to
spend an hour or more if the time is right. There are
several small cafes here (you will arrive about lunch time)
including an Italian Pizza place and Miguel's, a Mexican-
American establishment. Ione also offers an outstanding B& B
- the Heirloom at 214 Shakeley Lane. This 6 room historic
Southern Colonial Inn was erected by a Virginia transplant
in 1863 and features gardens, a Royal Breakfast and hospitality. It was first known as Creekside House, since it
faced Sutter Creek; it still does.

From here, proceed on SR 124 about 8 miles to its intersection with SR 49. Turn right on SR 49 only some 3 miles to
Plymouth (the overnight stop). There is a very nice new
Best Western Motel here (the Shenandoah Inn 800-542-4545;
call ahead for reservations). There is a swimming pool so
bring a bathing suit, (it is likely to be HOT). In town the
Plymouth House (B & B) on Main Street offers a certain old
fashioned ambience. The town of Plymouth itself is not
overly interesting. Originally known as Pokerville (or
sometimes Puckerville) the town was born in 1871, when the
Empire, Pacific and Plymouth Consolidated Gold Mines began
operations.

If there is time, and there should be, spend the rest of
the afternoon wandering around the Shenandoah Valley, to the
immediate east of town (it is well signed). There is a 20
mile loop (paved) road through the valley, passing through
Fiddletown (a quaint rustic, tree lined, one street town
with a variety of old buildings, including a Chinese Herb
Doctor's office and a general store.

FIDDLETOWN STORE

Mining started here in 1848 and the town was settled a year later. During the gold rush period, this town had the largest Chinese settlement outside of San Francisco. From 1872 to 1932, the town was renamed "Oleta" because a local judge was embarrassed by the previous name. This is somewhat of a tourist mecca and usually there are a number of them wandering around.

There are numerous wineries in the Shenandoah region, mostly scattered along Shenandoah Road and Steiner Way (see the map below). This area during the last fifteen years or so has become a major wine producing area and Amador County wines are rapidly increasing in stature (and price). Most of these operations are small, family oriented affairs, but most welcome visitors and offer tasting rooms and hospitality.

1   Sonny Grace Vineyards
2   Montevina Wines
3   Santino Winery
4   Deaver Vineyard
5   Charles Spinetta Winery
6   Amador Foothill Winery
7   Shenandoah Vineyards
8   TKC Vineyards
9   Karly
10 Story Winery
11 Baldinelli Vineyards
12 Vino Noceto

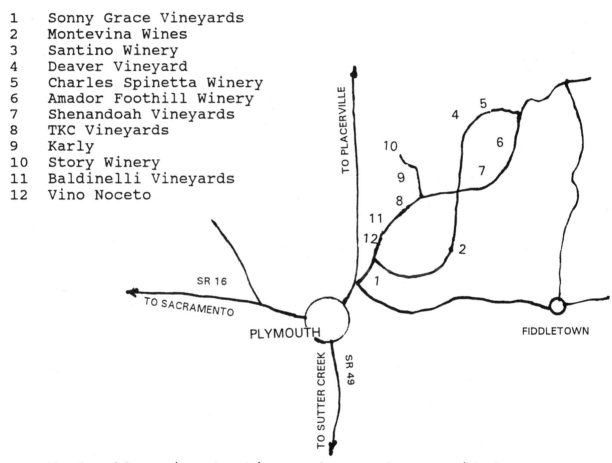

Most offer wine tasting and some have guided tours through the production facilities (at set hours). The tasting rooms are usually "quaint" but all have cool, high (and sometimes vaulted) ceilings and most offer original art, picture framing, books and ambience as well as vintage wines presumably without the middle man costs. The varieties and tastes are endless. Since it is impossible to cover them all, I would recommend: Charles Spinetta (closed Mondays) featuring Zinfandels, Cabernets and Chenin Blancs (both dry and sweet) and several dessert wines. A highlight is the wildlife art gallery. Shenandoah Vineyard is a small family estate begun in 1977 which has produced ten award winning wines. There is also a professional art gallery featuring contemporary art and ceramics. At Montevina, the largest and oldest winery in the county, they have recently embarked on an exciting program to feature various Italian wines such as Sangiovese, Nebbiolo, Aleatico, Refosco (and 40 others). They also make Barbera, Cabernet, Fume Blanc and the bold Zinfandels, Amador County's trademark.

The Sobon Estate (open daily) was founded in 1856 making it one of the oldest wineries in California. There is a spacious tasting room, historic cellars, lush landscaped gardens, a broad lawn and picnic areas. This is also the site of the Shenandoah Valley Museum (open daily 10-5).

The Museum includes a large collection of farm implements and furniture, a display of spinning equipment, the story of cooperage and how the wine industry began in the area. The museum is partially located in the original winery buildings erected in 1856.

The town of Plymouth has an old, interesting hotel, a number of shops including an old Chinese store and a fairly new bookstore- Heins, which houses 50,000 titles and ships books all over the world, especially to the Pacific Rim. There are also the ruins of the Plymouth-Empire Mine. Quartz mining and hard rock miners created Plymouth. By 1886, following a disastrous fire, the town contained 22 saloons and a race track (the present County Fair Grounds). The Plymouth Consolidated Mine employed 150 men, but in 1888 it closed down due to flooding. It remained idle until 1911, when it was sold and rebuilt, opening in 1913. It successfully operated until WW II when it closed, only to reopen in 1946, but ceased completely (and for good) in 1947. Total production was estimated at over $13.5 million.

This area was (and still is, to some extent) the center of the Slavic population of earlier California; many still reside here and there is even a Greek Orthodox Church and a Slavic cemetery still in operation in nearby Jackson. There are several good (really good) Italian restaurants in the vicinity, mostly strung along the old road to Sutters Creek about 6 miles to the south. These include Teresa's (closed Thursdays), and Buscaglias, an old speakeasy from the days when the area tolerated legal gaming (and illegal booze). The Bellotti Inn, in downtown Sutter Creek, established in 1858, features Italian family style dinners (closed Tuesdays). They are all popular.

The next morning, proceed on SR 49 south to Drytown. Actually it was not that "dry", since at one time there were more than 26 saloons located here. The first placer gold in the county was found here in 1848, making it one of the oldest camps on the Mother Lode; several of the oldest buildings still remain. Then 3 miles further to Amador City. This is the smallest incorporated "City" in California, both in terms of population and city size. Jose Maria Amador mined the creek in town from 1848 to 1849 and the town (and county) is named for him. Highway 49 bisects the community. The Amador Hotel (1850) and Imperial Hotel are prominent but there are other interesting buildings.

AMADOR CITY

2.5 miles further is Sutter Creek. In 1844 Capt. John Sutter sent some of his men into the Sierra foothills to locate timber for his "fort" on the American River in Sacramento. About 40 miles southeast of there they found a small forest of cedar and pine overlooking a pleasant valley bisected by a creek. They established a sawmill here, calling it Pine Woods, later to be renamed Tucker Hill. Sutter Creek must now be the "antique Capital" of the central Sierra and the main street provides many of these stores. All are fascinating; plan to spend at least 2 hours here- and probably more! In the old days this camp was among the larger mining towns. Close by is the famous Eureka Mine. Be sure to visit the Knight's Foundry, believed to be the last remaining water powered foundry in the United States. They now offer a special three day workshop in machine shop techniques and blacksmithing practices as practiced in the 1880's. There are a number of "Victorian" B & B's here including the Sutter Creek Inn, probably the original gold country inn.

Continue south about 4 miles to Jackson- which is the main "city" of the region and the County seat, with a current population of about 3,900. This camp was originally called "Bottileas" by the Mexicans, because of the many bottles found here. A Captain Weber and his party, searching the Stanislaus River for gold, found so much in so many places that the story of their success spread widely. Two great mines were located in this area- the Argonaut and the Kennedy. The old tailing wheels of the Kennedy Mine are still extant- in the Kennedy Tailing Wheels Park. It features a 68 foot wheel, picnic facilities, parking, the Mine Office and a kiosk depicting and narrating the history of the Kennedy Mine and the wheels. Erected in 1912, these wheels pumped the mine tailings out of the mine, over two hills to an impounding dam, thus preventing pollution of the creek. 75,000 gallons of water and tailings were removed daily; it makes an interesting side trip. This town also has many quaint shops, antique outlets, restaurants and places to see, including a Kitchen Shop which is well known for a hundred miles around. The old main street is quite picturesque and eminently "shopable" since the heavy traffic which used to go through here has been rerouted around the business district. Jackson also has a very good museum specializing in Mother Lode memorabilia. Highlights of the various exhibits are scale models of the Tailing Wheel headframe and the Kennedy Mine headframe. Working models clearly depict how all of this functions in producing and processing gold. The museum is located in one of the town's oldest houses, built in 1859. It has 15 exhibit rooms and is open Wednesday through Sunday 10-4.

From Jackson turn east on SR 88 some 10 miles to Pinegrove. Late in 1854, in a grove of tall pines, a pioneer built the Pinegrove House & Inn and in 1856 was named the first postmaster. It was located at the junction of stage roads to Jackson and Clinton. Nearby mines contributed to the area gold rush and many have been prospected ever since. At this point turn north on a signed road towards the little hamlet of Volcano. In a few miles is the Chaw Se Park, a 40 acre state park which preserves the local Miwok Indian culture. Central to the park is the grinding rock, a limestone outcropping 173 by 82 feet which is covered with hundreds of petroglyphs. It also has some 1100 mortar holes (known as chaw se's) which are the largest concentration in the state. These carved out cups were used to pulverize acorns and other nuts, seeds and berries. The park also contains recreated Indian structures, including a roundhouse (hung ge) which served as a gathering place for tribal, religious and social occasions. There are 21 campsites with tables and stoves. Piped water and restrooms are also available.

106

Continue on a few miles to Volcano, so named because the early settlers thought the land resembled a crater. Started in 1848, it was a lively mining camp, claiming a number of California "firsts": the first public library (1850), the first astronomical observatory site, the first private law school and the first little theater (The Volcano Thespian Society- 1854). Hydraulic mining began in 1895. There were originally 17 hotels in town, but only one -the historic two story St. George is still operating. There are other historic buildings, including a small museum. Many of the buildings are virtually in complete ruins, but enough stonework remains to indicate what must have been. This is a place to wander through leisurely. There are fascinating contrasts in textures and colors. The old General Store is worth a visit, as is the Hotel, which still serves excellent dinners and has a bar.

VOLCANO

Continue on through Volcano's main street, where the road veers left and goes up a rather steep grade (Rams Horn Grade), past Daffodil Hill, a fantasy garden spot which from about mid-March to Mid- April bursts forth with a waving sea of glowing daffodils, which now number over 300,000. This is a four acre farm in the same family since 1887. Initially it was a 36 acre ranch and toll road station for travelers and teamsters hauling timber from the high Sierra to the Jackson gold mines. The Hill is open from 9 to 5 during the season. Continue on to an intersection with the Fiddletown Road (Shakeridge Road), turn right here, following this road east to its intersection with SR 88. Turn left here and follow SR 88 back over the mountains to the point of origin.

FIDDLETOWN RELIC

VOLCANO RELIC

10

Reno/Sparks to Truckee, Sierraville, Yuba Pass, Sierra City, Downieville, Camptonville, San Juan, Nevada City (overnight), Grass Valley, Auburn, Donner Pass, Truckee and return.

This overnighter visits the northern mines of the Sierra Slope, centering on the area towns of Downieville, Nevada City and Grass Valley, with a possible two hour side trip to Auburn. All still have a distinct gold rush character, although they are all now rapidly expanding with retirement people, as indeed the entire west slope seems to be doing. The trip, as usual, begins and ends in the Reno-Sparks area. The trip west to Nevada City totals about 100 miles or about four hours of driving time. The return trip is somewhat shorter, due primarily to freeway speeds. All of it is on paved roads with available services at regular intervals. No special precautions are necessary. See the route map on the following page.

Take I-80 out of Reno the 37 miles to Truckee following the scenic Truckee River for most of the way. Turn north here on SR 89, (it is well signed), traveling the some 26 miles past Prosser Creek and Hobart Mills to Sierraville. This route follows the Little Truckee River for part of the way and then both Cottonwood and Cold Creeks for the remainder. Both are extremely scenic streams and there are developed Forest Service Campgrounds along the way. There are also many quakies (aspens) and cottonwoods lining the creek bottoms. Turn left in Sierraville, a small hamlet with many fine old historic buildings progressing four miles to and through the very small crossroads settlement of Sattley, to a well marked intersection with SR 49. The "Turner" barn, visible from the road, is well over 100 years old.

Turn left here, climbing a switchback up Turner Canyon to Yuba Pass (only 6,701 ft) where the Yuba Ski Area is located. Then another 14.3 miles past several campgrounds to an intersection with the road to Sardine Lakes, Salmon Lakes Parker Lakes and Gold Lake. This is the famous Lakes Basin Region where some 50 lakes provide a major summer recreational center. There is a traditional waystation here known as Bassetts, which has 3 housekeeping cabins, a cafe and some gas pumps which is open all year (not an easy effort; this is snowy high country in the wintertime). This place has been a rest stop, telegraph station, logging camp, sawmill and a supply point for well over 125 years. This is all very scenic country in a well wooded canyon that is steep, narrow and winding, following the river as it sparkles over the many boulders. There are several Forest Service campgrounds here, nestled among the trees.

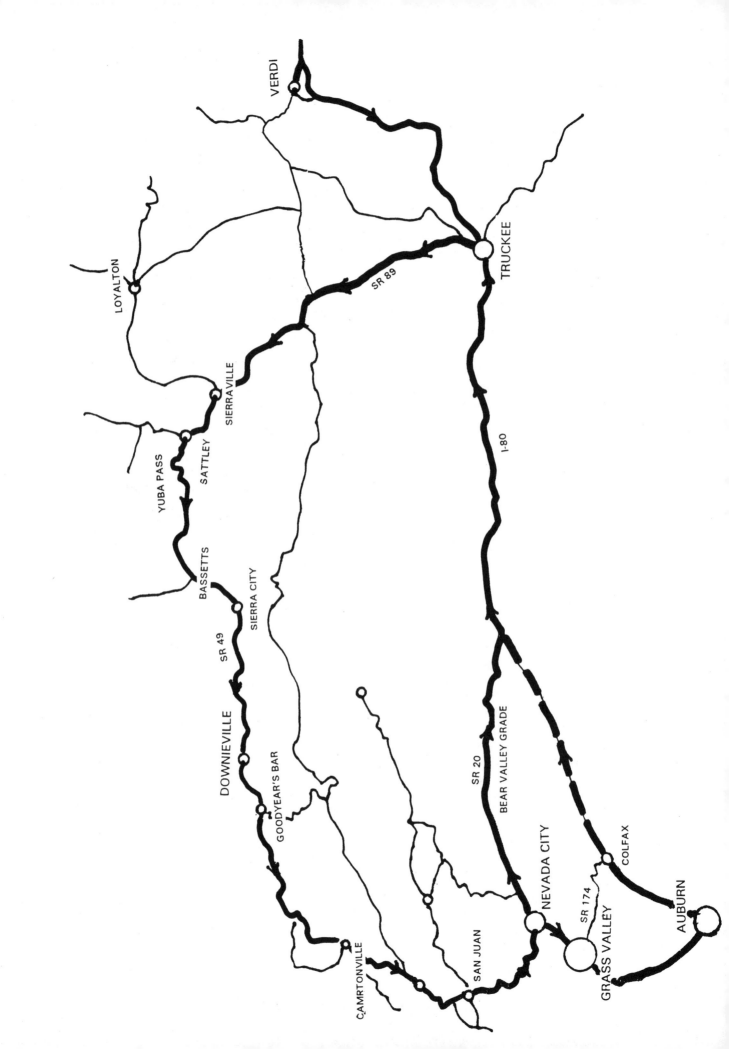

VERDI

LOYALTON

SR 89

TRUCKEE

I-80

SIERRAVILLE

YUBA PASS

SATTLEY

BASSETTS

SR 49

SIERRA CITY

SR 20

BEAR VALLEY GRADE

DOWNIEVILLE

GOODYEAR'S BAR

NEVADA CITY

COLFAX

SR 174

GRASS VALLEY

AUBURN

CAMRTONVILLE

SAN JUAN

Continue another four miles to a prominent sign indicating The Kentucky Mine and Museum. Turn off here (don't miss it) a short distance to this well equipped museum which features many artifacts of early day mining in the area and the best preserved stamp mill in the Sierra. There are many other ancient "irons" scattered about, such as the rusted donkey engine; see the photo below.

DONKEY ENGINE

The museum is open Wed-Sun from 10:00am to 5:00pm from Memorial Day through September and weekends only in October. There are guided stamp mill tours at 11:00, 1:00 and 3:00pm. There is also a pleasant place to sit in the shade and rest. The Sierra County Historical Society sponsors the Kennedy Mine Summer Concert Series each year. These concerts showcase a wide variety of musical styles including jazz, bluegrass, country swing, folk and classical as well as ethnic music from Ireland, Brazil and Scotland. These concerts are held every Friday evening from Memorial Day weekend until Labor Day weekend in the outdoor amphitheater.

A mile further is the quaint little town of Sierra City. Founded in 1850 by gold miners, it was soon destroyed by an avalanche during the winter of 1852-53. It was then rebuilt at a lower elevation and hasn't changed much since then. This is a funky one street town of perhaps 300 people with several cafes, a saloon or two and a number of gift stores catering to the rather little traffic on this transmountain highway. The natives boast that this is the last pristine (not their word) town left in California. I believe them (although Nevada City boasts the same thing). The old Wells Fargo building has been reconstructed and is now in use. A 141 pound gold nugget, taken from the Monumental Mine just out of town in 1869 is recorded as the second largest nugget found in California.

Then follow the Middle Fork of the Yuba River 12.6 miles past a number of small river frontage "resorts" such as Herrington's Sierra Pines (19 units, small golf course, restaurant and bar), The Lure Resort (8 housekeeping cabins), Sierra Shangri-La (11 housekeeping cabins, some with fireplaces) and Busch and Herringlakes Country Inn (4 rooms). This is an historic stage stop, begun in 1871 which also has a restaurant, a bar and whirlpool baths. Eventually this road leads to Downieville, the largest town in the area and the county seat of Sierra County. This town lies at the fork of the Yuba River and the Downie River and was named for Major Downie in 1849 following, as the rumor has it, a massive bribe of gold by the Major to most of the then citizens of the community. It was destroyed by fire on several occasions but always rebuilt. It was known as an exceptionally rich digging and reached a population of 5,000 at one time. A plaque on the main street tells it all. See the picture below.

DOWNIEVILLE

It's greatest and strangest claim to fame was that it was the only Mother Lode camp to have hung a woman! It seems that a certain Juanita, a Mexican "lady of the evening"

112

(although she was called a "dance hall girl"), was hung
from a bridge in 1851 following her stabbing of a well
known and liked local miner. The total story is more involved and more interesting but is too long for this re-
port. Get the full story (for $1.00) if you visit the
place. It is one of the prettiest towns in the Sierra,
nestled in the confluence of the two streams and surrounded
with well wooded mountains. The "downtown area" remains
much as it was in the last century with many old buildings
and board sidewalks and is easily walkable, since it is
quite compact. One of the more interesting buildings left
intact is the Craycroft Building, built in 1852 as a saloon. It currently houses YoHo (gold sales and a bakery).
Originally it had the longest (70 foot) single plank bar in
California. See the picture below.

DOWNIEVILLE STORE

    There is an information kiosk in the town center which
can supply information and maps as needed. There is also a
museum here, one of the finest on the 49er Trail. It is
open from Memorial Day to the first weekend in October.
There are a number of motels in town which include: Coyote
Cabins (7 units), Crandalls Riverside Motel (8 units),
Downieville Motor Inn (12 units), Robinson's Motel (8
units) and Saundra Dyer's Resort (10 rooms and 4 cottages)
and a swimming pool.

    By the mid 1850's Downieville, boasted a population
making it one of the largest towns in California, surpassed
only by San Francisco, Sacramento, Grass Valley and Nevada
City. It missed becoming the state capitol by ten votes.
Until 1860 all supplies were brought here by mule trains,
which sometimes involved as many as 75 animals. There were
no roads then wide enough for wagons.

From here it is 3 1/2 miles to Goodyear's Bar, a small collection of older houses bordering the river a mile or so off the highway. Then 8.3 miles to Indian Hill where there is a road north to Brandy City. Then it is a few miles to the old town of Camptonville. All that is left here now is a collection of quiet homes, a post office and a monument to a Mr. Pelton, the inventor of the Pelton Overshot Water-wheel, a device much used in the early mines. Continue on 5.2 miles through North Columbia to a road to the left which is (marked) to the Malakoff Diggins. This was once the site of the world's largest hydraulic operation. This activity peaked between the 1850's and the 1880's when water, brought by flumes and ditches, was projected against the red hill-sides through giant nozzles (called Monitors) which were capable of hurling 50 pound boulders up to 200 feet. This area produced some 3.5 million dollars in gold, but was closed down by a State edict due to the damage being done to downstream rivers and waterways. Two miles further is North San Juan. This town has the "old look", with large old brick buildings, some with iron grillwork. This was the business center of the hydraulic mining efforts.

It is then only 14.9 miles on into Nevada City which is the designated "turn-around" point. This is the County Seat of Sierra County and in the early days was a busy mining center, producing placer gold worth eight million dollars. Many old landmarks remain such as the assay office, the old firehouse and the meeting hall. This town is (rightfully) called "the most complete gold town left in California". It is indeed a sort of "living museum". In 1849 the first cabin was built at a point where Gold Run Creek flowed into Deer Creek in which a Dr. A.B..Caldwell established a store. By March 1850 the population had increased to the point that a city government was elected and the name "Nevada" chosen. Most of the buildings in the downtown historic district date from 1864 when the area was rebuilt after a disastrous fire in November of 1863. The dominant architectural theme is Victorian commercial style although the false fronted vernacular style is also seen.

NEVADA CITY

114

Most buildings had balconies or shed canopies over the sidewalks. Since 1917 the business district has remained intact, and the whole area is now subject to very stringent architectural controls (exercised by the City) to insure the maintenance of the "Mother Lode" character of this old town. The old assay office was the starting place for the stampede to Nevada and the Comstock Lode and this office assayed the first ore from Virginia City. There are a number of motels, lodges and B&B's in town as well as the old and historic National Hotel. This is the oldest hotel in continuous operation west of the Mississippi River. The original hotel was erected in 1863; it was destroyed by fire in 1880, but rebuilt the same year. One of the better motels is the Northern Queen Inn at 400 Railroad Avenue (916-265-5824). This quiet and "romantic" facility is nestled along Gold Run Creek (a pound of gold per day was taken from this creek during the gold rush) and there are "Chalets" and "cottages" available for larger parties. There is, of course, a heated swimming pool, a spa and a restaurant. The many shops in town are most interesting and it is easily possible to spend several hours wandering the main street. There are a number of interesting dining spots including Cirines (which seemed to have most of the action, particularly among the younger set; it is Italian in preference), and the National Hotel at 2 Broad Street (the main avenue) which has an excellent (local) chef who is quite accomplished.

Six miles further on SR49 is the slightly larger town of Grass Valley. In 1849 a party of emigrants, searching for strayed cattle, discovered a luxuriant, grassy stretch of land between several forested hills. It immediately became known as "Grassy". In August of that year five men built a cabin here and became the first permanent settlers. In the spring of 1850 more prospectors arrived and by 1851 there were 150 wooden structures including the usual saloons, hotels and stores.

GRASS VALLEY

Hardrock mining was the only method and miners familiar with these techniques had to be imported from Cornwall. Irish laborers also came, but a bit later. These two labor forces combined to make Grass Valley the largest mining town in the state. In November 1852, for instance, 1300 votes were cast, ranking this place as the 7th largest town in the state; larger than Los Angeles, San Diego and Oakland. In September 1853, fire destroyed 300 buildings within two hours. But it was quickly rebuilt (with bricks this time) and it has continued to grow ever since. This beautifully situated town was once the home of Lola Montez, the famous dancer and her tame bear (the bear was the tamer of the two) and of Lotta Crabtree, a singer who performed before the crowned heads of Europe. The Empire Star Mine is the oldest, richest hardrock mine in California. It began in 1850 and lasted until 1956. 3.8 million ounces of gold were retrieved from the 367 miles of underground shafts and tunnels. It is now a 777 acre State Park, offering extensive hiking trails, biking and picnicking as well as a closeup look at what mining was in those days.

At this point a decision has to be made regarding the return trip. For those who are short of time, the quickest and easiest is to return through Nevada City on SR 49, diverting to SR 20, which heads 28 miles almost due east through Bear Valley to a connection to I-80 above Emigrant Gap, where there is then a high speed 63 mile run directly into Reno, for a total length of 91 miles. For those who wish to dawdle a bit more, take SR 174 out of Grass Valley 12 miles to I-80 at Colfax, where there is then (again) a high speed connection to Reno- a total trip of about 102 miles. For those who wish to see yet another old foothill gold town, proceed on SR 49 the 24 miles to Auburn. This was a rich camp at one time, first known as Wood's Dry Diggins. This road is somewhat congested, especially the ten miles or so coming into Auburn. As you approach the town, cross over the freeway, proceeding to the signal where a right turn will go past the Old Courthouse on the Hill and then down Lincoln Way (old US 40) into "Old Town". Old Auburn once had many Chinese; even today their descendants still live there. Of special interest here is the Placer-Herald newspaper, serving the County since 1852, the Auburn Hook and Ladder Co. organized in 1852 and the Orleans Hotel, built in 1852 and rebuilt after the great fire of 1855. Park where you can and spend another hour or so wandering around here. It is not quite as attractive as the previous towns but it worth some time, perhaps to have lunch.

From here it is a simple right turn into the adjacent freeway and again the rather dull trip back to Reno-Sparks. This alternative involves a total trip length of 131 miles.

116

Since Truckee can't be avoided in any case, an additional hour or so can be well spent investigating the many fine stores in that town. The first white settler here was Joseph Grey who built Grey's Station in 1863. The community bloomed when logging began following the erection of the first lumber mill in 1867. The town's name was then changed to Coburn Station and later in 1868 again changed to Truckee, during the rebuilding following a major fire. Also in 1868 the first train arrived on the newly constructed Central Pacific tracks and Truckee quickly became the second largest Chinatown on the west coast due to the many thousands of Chinese employed to construct this railroad. Another industry arrived about this same time, ice harvesting, and it played a major role for the next 60 years. The end of this came in the 1920's when mechanical refrigeration supplanted it. This old town has, during the last 25 years or so, become a major tourist (winter and summer) recreation area. Truckee has a surprising number of art galleries, interesting eating (and drinking) houses and shops of all kinds, including the Truckee Ice Cream parlor (since 1948), an old time counter serving all sorts of ice cream treats.

　　　Raymond M. Smith was the Director of the Regional
Planning Commission of Reno, Sparks and Washoe County from
1950 to 1960 and since then a planning and design consult-
ant to ten northern Nevada Counties. He is also an experienced camper, explorer and historian of Northern Nevada,
especially the Black Rock Country and the western valleys.
Author of four Nevada History books to date. He is a
graduate of Stanford University and Harvard University and
has four native sons, all still living in the state.

118